# SUGAR & SPICE

First published in Great Britain in 2026
by Hamlyn, an imprint of
Octopus Publishing Group Ltd
Carmelite House
50 Victoria Embankment
London EC4Y 0DZ

www.octopusbooks.co.uk

An Hachette UK Company
www.hachette.co.uk

The authorized representative in the EEA is
Hachette Ireland, 8 Castlecourt Centre,
Dublin 15, D15 XTP3, Ireland (email: info@hbgi.ie)



Distributed in the US by Hachette Book Group
1290 Avenue of the Americas, 4th and 5th Floors
New York, NY 10104

Distributed in Canada by Canadian Manda Group
664 Annette St., Toronto, Ontario, Canada M6S 2C8



ISBN: 978-0-60064-029-5
eISBN: 978-0-60064-039-4

A CIP catalogue record for this book is available from the British Library.

Printed and bound in China.

10 9 8 7 6 5 4 3 2 1

Publisher: Lucy Pessell
Senior Designer: Alicia House
Senior Editor: Katie Button
Assistant Editor: Samina Rahman
Production Manager: Allison Gonsalves

**Picture Acknowledgements**
Photography: Octopus Publishing Group

MIX
Paper | Supporting responsible forestry
FSC www.fsc.org FSC® C008047

**Publisher's Note**

Standard level spoon measurement are used in all recipes.
1 tablespoon = one 15 ml spoon
1 teaspoon = one 5 ml spoon

Both imperial and metric measurements have been given in all recipes. Use one set of measurements only and not a mixture of both.

Eggs should be medium unless otherwise stated. The Department of Health advises that eggs should not be consumed raw. This book contains dishes made with raw or lightly cooked eggs. It is prudent for more vulnerable people such as pregnant and nursing mothers, invalids, the elderly, babies and young children to avoid uncooked or lightly cooked dishes made with eggs. Once prepared these dishes should be kept refrigerated and used promptly.

Milk should be full fat unless otherwise stated. Butter should be unsalted unless otherwise stated.

Slow cookers and ovens should be preheated to the specific temperature – if using a fan-assisted oven, follow manufacturer's instructions for adjusting the time and the temperature.

This book includes dishes made with nuts and nut derivatives. It is advisable for those with known allergic reactions to nuts and nut derivatives and those who may be potentially vulnerable to these allergies, such as pregnant and nursing mothers, invalids, the elderly, babies and children, to avoid dishes made with nuts and nut oils. It is also prudent to check the labels of preprepared ingredients for the possible inclusion of nut derivatives.

Vegetarians should look for the 'V' symbol on a cheese to ensure it is made with vegetarian rennet.

Vegans should check for vegan labelling on dark chocolate to ensure that it is made without the use of animal products.

FRANCESCA HUNTINGDON

# SUGAR & SPICE

## Sweet Treats and Bakes to Enjoy as the Nights Draw In

hamlyn

# CONTENTS

6 INTRODUCTION

8 PASTRIES, PIES & TARTS

54 MUFFINS, CUPCAKES & LOAVES

94 BISCUITS, BROWNIES & TRAYBAKES

138 LITTLE TREATS

154 PUDDINGS & DESSERTS

212 SHOWSTOPPERS

240 INDEX

# INTRODUCTION

The nights are drawing in, there's a chill in the air and we're craving the cozy warmth of blankets and the crackle and glow of a fire. These are the times to hunker down and seek comfort but they're also the celebration seasons – an opportunity to bring friends and family together and share a slice of something indulgent.

The smell of apples bubbling with spice or the crack of pastry as a fork nudges it conjure the kitchens of our childhoods – the oven door opening and filling the air with buttery warmth, recipes scribbled by hand and the comforting cadence of seasonal cooking. Dessert somehow feels less of an indulgence and more a ritual of care.

Traybakes brimming with marshmallows and caramelized nuts, stacks of sticky cinnamon buns and tins of cookies, cupcakes and brownies are handed over on doorsteps and tables are adorned with show-stopping cakes and centrepiece bakes.

And there is chocolate. So. Much. Chocolate.

*Sugar & Spice* is a treasure trove of more than 100 all-things-nice recipes with classics such as **SWEET CHERRY PIES** and **GINGERED TREACLE TART** nestled among twists such as **MARSALA RAISIN COFFEE MUFFINS** and **CLOVE & CARDAMOM COOKIES**.

# PASTRIES, PIES & TARTS

# Sticky Cinnamon & Pecan Buns

*Makes:* 10
*Prep time*: 45 minutes, plus standing and proving
*Cook time*: 30 minutes

- 1 tablespoon ground flaxseed
- 200 ml (7 fl oz) almond milk
- 15 g (½ oz) fast-action dried yeast
- 450 g (14½ oz) strong white bread flour, plus extra for dusting
- ½ teaspoon salt
- 75 g (3 oz) softened butter, cubed
- 50 g (2 oz) soft light brown sugar
- 125 g (4 oz) icing (confectioners') sugar
- sunflower oil, for oiling

**FOR THE FILLING**

- 100 g (4 oz) softened butter
- 8 tablespoons soft light brown sugar
- 2 teaspoons ground cinnamon
- 75 g (3 oz) pecan nuts, roughly chopped
- 6 fresh Medjool dates, stoned (pitted) and mashed
- 2 tablespoons maple syrup

Mix the flaxseed with 3 tablespoons of water and set aside. Heat the milk gently in a saucepan until lukewarm, then stir in the yeast and leave to stand for 10 minutes.

Mix the flour and salt in a large bowl, add the butter and combine until the mixture resembles breadcrumbs, then stir in the brown sugar.

Combine the flaxseed and yeast mixtures together, then stir into the flour mixture to make a smooth, soft dough. Tip the dough onto a lightly floured surface and knead for about 5 minutes until smooth and elastic. Put it in a clean bowl, cover with clingfilm (plastic wrap) and leave to rise in a warm place for 10 minutes.

Make the filling. Mix the butter, sugar and cinnamon in a bowl until well combined, then add the pecans, dates and maple syrup.

Turn the dough out onto a lightly floured surface and knead for 2 minutes until smooth. Roll out to a rectangle about 30 x 45 cm (12 x 18 inches). Spread the filling evenly across it, then roll tightly from one of the long sides to form a spiralled log. Slice into 10 even slices, then place well spaced on a baking sheet, cover loosely with lightly oiled clingfilm and leave to prove in a warm place for 30 minutes.

Remove the clingfilm. Bake in a preheated oven, 200°C (400°F), Gas Mark 6, for 25 minutes until golden. Leave to cool on a wire rack. Put the icing sugar in a bowl, add 2 tablespoons of water and mix until soft and smooth. Drizzle over the cooled buns and leave to set before serving.

# APPLE FRITTERS

VG

*Serves:* 4 – 6
*Prep time:* 20 minutes, plus standing
*Cook time:* 20 minutes

3 apples, peeled and cored
200 g (7 oz) plain (all-purpose) flour
1 teaspoon baking powder
1½ tablespoons caster (superfine) sugar
1 teaspoon vanilla extract (optional)
200 ml (7 fl oz) dairy-free milk
flavourless oil, for deep-frying
2 tablespoons icing (confectioners') sugar

Slice the apples 1 cm (½ inch) thick and set aside.

Use a whisk to combine the flour, baking powder and caster sugar in a bowl. Slowly add the vanilla extract, if using, and milk and whisk until you have a smooth batter.

Bring the oil to 170°C (340°F) in a deep saucepan or wok. If you don't have a thermometer, carefully drop in a little batter: it should sizzle, but not turn golden immediately. Dip the apple slices into the batter, coating well, then lower straight into the oil (taking care to not burn yourself – use a fork or tongs) and cook for 2–3 minutes until golden and puffy. You will need to cook them in smallish batches of 3–4 at a time, to avoid overcrowding the pan.

Remove with a slotted spoon and drain on kitchen paper (paper towel). Sift the icing sugar over the top and serve immediately.

# BANANA FRITTERS

VG

*Serves:* 4
*Prep time:* 20 minutes, plus standing
*Cook time:* 5 minutes

225 g (7½ oz) plain (all-purpose) flour
½ teaspoon ground nutmeg
2 teaspoons ground cinnamon
375 ml (13 fl oz) sparkling water
sunflower oil, for deep-frying
4 bananas, halved lengthways and widthways
3 tablespoons demerara sugar
1 tablespoon caster (superfine) sugar

Mix the flour, nutmeg and 1 teaspoon of the cinnamon together in a bowl, then make a well in the centre. Gradually whisk in enough of the sparkling water to make a smooth batter thick enough to coat the back of a spoon. Leave to stand for 20 minutes.

Fill a deep-sided saucepan one-third full with oil and heat to 180–190°C (350–375°F), or until a cube of bread browns in 30 seconds.

Using tongs, dip the banana pieces into the batter, then gently lower into the hot oil and cook in batches for 30 seconds–1 minute until golden and crisp, taking care not to overcrowd the pan, as they will stick together and the oil temperature will drop.

Remove with a slotted spoon and drain on kitchen paper (paper towel).

Mix the sugars with the remaining cinnamon, then scatter over the hot fritters and serve immediately.

# QUICK CHURROS

(VG)

*Serves:* 4
*Prep time:* 10 minutes
*Cook time:* 4–6 minutes

1 teaspoon ground cinnamon
100 g (3½ oz) granulated sugar
100 g (3½ oz) dark chocolate, broken into squares
4 slices of stale white sliced bread
4 tablespoons vegan butter

In a shallow bowl, mix together the cinnamon and sugar. Set aside.

Melt the chocolate in 30-second blasts in the microwave on high until smooth. Set aside.

Slice the bread into thick strips.

Heat 2 tablespoons of the butter in a large frying pan (skillet) and cook half the bread strips for 1–2 minutes on each side until toasty and golden. Remove from the pan, add straight to the cinnamon sugar bowl and toss to coat.

Repeat with the remaining butter and bread strips. Serve dunked in the melted chocolate.

# HONEY HALVA GRIWECH

*Makes:* 20
*Prep time:* 30 minutes
*Cook time:* 15 minutes

150 g (5 oz) white sesame seeds
1 packet fast-action dried yeast
1 kg (2 lb) plain (all-purpose) flour
4 teaspoons baking powder
½ teaspoon ground turmeric
pinch of saffron
350 ml (12 fl oz) of a mixture of melted butter and sunflower oil
3 tablespoons vinegar
oil, for deep frying

## FOR THE GLAZE

375 ml (13 fl oz) clear honey
150 ml (¼ pint) orange-flower water

Toast sesame seeds in a frying pan (skillet) over a low heat. Remove and leave to cool.

Mix the yeast in a bowl with a little warm water. Tip the flour into a large bowl, make a hollow in the centre and add in all the other ingredients except the oil. Knead the dough thoroughly, then roll out and cut into 10 x 8 cm (4 x 3½ inch) rectangles, 2.5 cm (1 inch) thick. Twist the rectangles and join the two ends.

Heat the oil in a deep-fat fryer or deep-sided frying pan and fry the cakes in batches until golden on all sides.

Meanwhile, make the glaze. Heat the honey with the orange-flower water in a saucepan. Dip the hot halva in the glaze, then sprinkle with the sesame seeds.

VG

# Speedy Cinnamon Rolls

*Serves:* 2
*Prep time:* 10–15 minutes
*Cook time:* 2–3 minutes

1 banana

12 tablespoons plain (all-purpose) flour, plus extra for dusting

2 teaspoons baking powder

1–4 tablespoons dairy-free milk

2 tablespoons granulated sugar

1 teaspoon ground cinnamon

1 tablespoon vegan butter, melted

### FOR THE GLAZE

100 g (3½ oz) icing (confectioners') sugar

1–2 tablespoons dairy-free milk

In a large bowl, mash the banana with a fork, then add the flour, baking powder and milk and bring together into a thick, slightly tacky dough.

Lightly flour a work surface and push the dough out with your hands until you have a thick rectangle about 20 x 30 cm (8 x 12 inches) large.

Combine the sugar and cinnamon, then brush the dough with the melted butter and sprinkle the cinnamon sugar on top. Roll up tightly from one long edge to make a spiralled log.

Slice the log into 5–6 pieces and nestle the rolls into 2 mugs or a small microwave-safe dish. Microwave on high for 2–3 minutes if in a single dish, or 1 minute 30 seconds for each mug, until puffy and golden.

Meanwhile, make the glaze. Mix together the icing sugar and milk until you have a smooth dropping consistency. Pour over the cinnamon rolls and enjoy.

# Cinnamon Doughnuts

*Makes:* 10
*Prep time:* 10–15 minutes, plus proving
*Cook time:* 3 minutes

### FOR THE DOUGH

450 g (14½ oz) strong white bread flour, plus extra for dusting

1¼ teaspoons fast-action dried yeast

25 g (1 oz) unsalted butter, softened

50 g (2 oz) caster (superfine) sugar

1 large egg, beaten

225 ml (7½ fl oz) milk

2 teaspoons vanilla extract

½ teaspoon salt

### TO FINISH

100 g (3½ oz) caster (superfine) sugar

1 teaspoon ground cinnamon

sunflower oil, for deep-frying

### TO SERVE

strawberry jam (jelly) (optional)

whipped cream (optional)

Mix the flour and yeast in a bowl, and rub in the butter. Then stir in the sugar, egg, milk, vanilla extract and salt and mix into a soft dough. Turn the dough out onto a lightly floured surface and knead for 5–8 minutes.

Cut the dough into 10 equal pieces. Shape each into a ball and space them well apart on a large, greased baking sheet. Cover loosely with oiled clingfilm (plastic wrap) and leave to rise in a warm place for 30–40 minutes, or until almost doubled in size.

Mix together the sugar and cinnamon on a plate. Heat 8 cm (3 inches) of oil in a large saucepan until a small piece of bread dropped into the oil sizzles on the surface and turns pale golden in about 30 seconds.

Fry the doughnuts, 3–4 at a time, for about 3 minutes, turning them once until golden on both sides. Remove with a slotted spoon and drain onto several sheets of kitchen paper (paper towel). Cook the remainder. Roll the doughnuts in the cinnamon sugar while still warm. Serve immediately with strawberry jam and whipped cream, if liked.

# Apricot & Pistachio Purses

*Makes:* 8
*Prep time:* 25 minutes, plus chilling
*Cook time:* 15 minutes

- 75 g (3 oz) butter, at room temperature
- 25 g (1 oz) caster (superfine) sugar
- a few drops of almond essence or orange flower water
- 1 small egg yolk
- 25 g (1 oz) ground almonds (almond meal)
- 25 g (1 oz) pistachio nuts, roughly chopped
- 8 apricots
- 4 sheets of filo pastry, 48 × 23 cm (19 × 9 inches), defrosted if frozen
- icing (confectioners') sugar, for dusting

Cream 25 g (1 oz) of the butter with the sugar and almond essence or orange flower water until light and pale. Add the egg yolk and ground almonds, mix until smooth, then stir in the pistachios. Chill for 15 minutes.

Cut each apricot in half, remove the stones, then sandwich the apricots back together with the pistachio mixture in the middle.

Melt the remaining butter. Unfold the pastry sheets and put one sheet on your work surface. Brush with melted butter, then cut into 4 rectangles. Put an apricot on one of the rectangles, lift up the corners of the pastry to enclose the apricot, then pinch together at the top of the fruit. Wrap with a second pastry rectangle at right angles to the first to form a purse shape. Repeat with the remaining apricots and pastry sheets, then place on a baking sheet.

Brush with a little of the remaining butter. Bake in a preheated oven, 190°C (375°F), Gas Mark 5, for 15 minutes until golden. Dust with icing sugar and serve warm or cold with vanilla ice cream.

# APPLE & HAZELNUT FILOS

*Makes:* 12

*Prep time:* 10 minutes

*Cook time:* 15 minutes

125 g (4 oz) unsalted butter

5 dessert apples, peeled, cored and sliced into thin wedges

2 tablespoons dark soft brown sugar

1½ teaspoons lemon juice

3 sheets of filo pastry, about 30 x 40 cm (12 x 16 inches)

2 tablespoons roasted chopped hazelnuts

warmed toffee sauce, to drizzle (optional)

Melt the butter in a large frying pan (skillet) and pour one-third of it into a small dish. Add the apples, sugar and lemon juice to the pan and cook over a medium heat for 7–8 minutes, turning occasionally, until tender and golden. Set aside.

Meanwhile, brush each filo sheet with the reserved melted butter and lay the 3 sheets on top of one another. Cut the stacked sheets into 12 squares, then use these to line a 12-hole bun tray, arranging them at slightly different angles.

Bake in a preheated oven, 220°C (425°F), Gas Mark 7, for 7–8 minutes until crisp and golden.

Arrange the filo pastry cases on serving plates and fill with the caramelized apples and roasted hazelnuts. Serve with warm toffee sauce, if liked.

# SPICED HAZELNUT PALMIERS

*Makes:* 30–40

*Prep time:* 10 minutes

*Cook time:* 23 minutes

50 g (2 oz) whole blanched hazelnuts

1½ teaspoons ground cinnamon

¼ teaspoon ground nutmeg

¾ teaspoon ground ginger

3 tablespoons demerara sugar

375 g (12 oz) chilled ready-rolled puff pastry

50 g (2 oz) unsalted butter, melted

icing (confectioners') sugar, for dusting

Dry-fry the hazelnuts in a large, frying pan (skillet) over a medium–low heat for 4–5 minutes, shaking frequently, until lightly toasted. Tip into a food processor with the spices and blend until finely chopped. Place the sugar in a bowl and stir in the nuts.

Unroll the pastry on a clean surface and brush lightly with some of the melted butter. Sprinkle over the nut mixture, then roll the long sides of the pastry into the centre. Cut into 30–40 x 1 cm (½ inch) slices and place on 2 large baking sheets with nonstick baking paper. Brush with the remaining butter.

Bake in a preheated oven, 220°C (425°F), Gas Mark 7, for 10 minutes, then remove from the oven and turn the palmiers over. Return to the oven for a further 5–8 minutes until puffed up and golden. Transfer to wire racks to cool. Serve dusted with icing sugar.

# Gâteau Pithiviers with Plums

*Serves:* 6
*Prep time:* 30 minutes
*Cook time:* 25–30 minutes

- 100 g (3½ oz) unsalted butter, at room temperature
- 100 g (3½ oz) caster (superfine) sugar
- 100 g (3½ oz) ground almonds (almond meal)
- a few drops of almond essence
- 1 egg, beaten, plus extra to glaze
- 500 g (1 lb) chilled ready-made puff pastry
- 375 g (12 oz) plums, pitted and thickly sliced
- icing (confectioners') sugar, for dusting

Cream the butter and sugar together in a bowl until pale and smooth. Add the ground almonds and almond essence, then the egg, and mix together until smooth.

Roll out half the pastry thinly on a lightly floured surface and trim to a 25 cm (10 inch) circle using a dinner plate as a guide. Place on a wetted baking sheet, then spread the almond paste over the top, leaving a 2.5 cm (1 inch) border of pastry around the edges. Arrange the plums in a single layer on top. Brush the pastry border with a little beaten egg.

Roll out the remaining pastry thinly and trim to a circle a little larger than the first. Cut 5 or 6 swirly 'S' shapes out of the centre of the pastry, then lift the pastry circle over a rolling pin and position on the almond paste. Press the edges together to seal and trim to neaten if needed. Knock up the edge by gently tapping a sharp knife around the edge to separate the pastry layers slightly, then flute the edges by pressing the first and second finger on to the pastry edge, then make small cuts with a knife between them to create a scalloped edge. Repeat all the way around.

Brush the top with beaten egg. Bake in a preheated oven, 200°C (400°F), Gas Mark 6, for 25–30 minutes until well risen and golden.

Leave to cool slightly, then dust with icing sugar and serve cut into wedges with cream.

# PLUM TURNOVERS

*Makes:* 6
*Prep time:* 10 minutes
*Cook time:* 20 minutes

320 g (10¾ oz) ready-rolled puff pastry
150 g (5 oz) shop-bought custard
1 tablespoon soft light brown sugar
1 teaspoon ground cinnamon
2 tablespoons ground almonds (almond meal)
1 teaspoon finely grated orange rind, plus extra to garnish
5 plums, stoned (pitted) and thinly sliced
1 small egg, beaten
demerara sugar, to sprinkle
sweetened mascarpone, to serve (optional)

Unroll the pastry and cut it into 6 x 10 cm (4 inch) squares. Place on a baking sheet lined with baking paper and spread the custard over them, leaving a 1 cm (½ inch) border around the edges.

Put the brown sugar in a bowl with the cinnamon, ground almonds and orange rind and mix well. Add the plums and toss to coat, then arrange in a diagonal row across each pastry square.

Brush the border with beaten egg, then bring 2 diagonally opposite corners together and press to seal. Brush the pastries with the remaining egg and sprinkle 1 teaspoon demerara sugar over each one. Bake in a preheated oven, 200°C (400°F), Gas Mark 6, for 15–20 minutes until the pastry is crisp and golden. Serve warm with sweetened mascarpone garnished with grated orange rind, if desired.

# DATE CRESCENTS

*Makes:* 40
*Prep time:* 30 minutes
*Cook time:* 15 minutes

## FOR THE PASTRY

500 g (1 lb) plain (all-purpose) flour
pinch of baking powder
125 g (4 oz) granulated sugar
250 g (8 oz) butter, melted

## FOR THE FILLING

250 g (8 oz) date paste (or use stoned/pitted, chopped dates)
knob of butter
½ teaspoon cinnamon
125 g (4 oz) icing (confectioners') sugar

Make the pastry. Mix all the ingredients together to form a dough. Leave it to rest while you make the filling.

In a bowl, mix all the ingredients for the filling together and form into 40 balls the size of a hazelnut.

Form the pastry into 40 balls the size of a walnut. Press a ball of filling into each one, close the pastry around it, then fashion it into the shape of a crescent.

Place on an oiled baking sheet. Bake in a preheated oven, 150°C (300°F), Gas Mark 2, for 15 minutes. Remove from the oven and dredge each crescent through the icing sugar to coat on all sides.

# TOFFEE CHOUX BUNS

*Makes:* 8
*Prep time:* 30 minutes, plus cooling
*Cook time:* 45 minutes

50 g (2 oz) butter

150 ml (¼ pint) sparkling water

1 tablespoon golden caster (superfine) sugar

65 g (2½ oz) plain (all-purpose) flour, sifted

2 eggs, lightly beaten

### FOR THE TOPPING

200 g (7 oz) plain dark chocolate

75 g (3 oz) butter

### FOR THE FILLING

300 ml (½ pint) double (heavy) cream

1 teaspoon vanilla extract

1 teaspoon golden caster (superfine) sugar

8 tablespoons dulce de leche or thick caramel sauce

Melt the butter with the sparkling water and sugar in a heavy-based saucepan. Bring to the boil, turn off the heat and immediately tip in all the flour. Beat vigorously with a wooden spoon until the mixture forms a ball in the centre of the pan. Tip the ball into a bowl and cool for 15 minutes. Whisk in the eggs gradually until the mixture is smooth and glossy.

Sprinkle water over a nonstick baking sheet. Put 8 large spoonfuls of the mixture, well spaced apart, onto the baking sheet. Bake in a preheated oven, 220°C (425°F), Gas Mark 7, for 30 minutes until risen and golden brown, then turn off the oven. Pierce each bun with a sharp knife to let the steam escape and leave in the oven for 10–15 minutes to dry out. Transfer to a wire rack and cool completely.

To make the topping, melt the chocolate with the butter in a bowl over a pan of simmering water, ensuring the bowl does not touch the water.

Use a serrated knife to cut the choux buns in half. Make the filling. Whip the cream with the vanilla extract and sugar. Spread a spoonful of dulce de leche or caramel sauce into the base of each bun and top with a spoonful of whipped cream and the choux bun lids. Spoon the melted chocolate on top.

# Gingered Profiteroles

*Makes:* 20
*Prep time:* 35 minutes, plus cooling
*Cook time:* 20 minutes

150 ml (¼ pint) water
50 g (2 oz) unsalted butter
pinch of salt
65 g (2½ oz) plain (all-purpose) flour, sifted
2 eggs
½ teaspoon vanilla extract
250 ml (8 fl oz) double (heavy) cream
50 g (2 oz) crystallized or glacé ginger, finely chopped

## For the sauce

150 g (5 oz) plain dark chocolate, broken into pieces
150 ml (¼ pint) milk
50 g (2 oz) caster (superfine) sugar
2 tablespoons brandy

Pour the measurement water into a medium saucepan, add the butter and salt and heat until the butter has melted. Bring up to the boil, then take off the heat and stir in the flour. Put the pan back on the heat and cook briefly, stirring until the mixture makes a smooth ball. Leave to cool.

Beat the eggs and vanilla extract together, then gradually beat into the flour mixture until smooth. Spoon the mixture into a large piping bag fitted with a 1.5 cm (¾ inch) plain nozzle. Lightly grease a large baking sheet, then pipe on 20 balls, leaving space between them.

Bake in a preheated oven, 200°C (400°F), Gas Mark 6, for 15 minutes until well risen. Make a slit in the side of each ball for the steam to escape, return to the turned-off oven for 5 minutes, then transfer to a wire rack and cool completely.

Make the sauce. Heat the chocolate, milk and sugar in a saucepan, stirring until smooth. Take off the heat and mix in the brandy.

Whip the cream until it forms soft peaks, fold in the ginger, then enlarge the slit in each profiterole and spoon in the ginger cream. Pile onto serving dishes and drizzle with the sauce.

# APPLE & BLACKBERRY STRUDELS

*Serves:* 4

*Prep time:* 10 minutes

*Cook time:* 20 minutes

3 Granny Smith apples, peeled, cored and thinly sliced

125 g (4 oz) blackberries

100 g (3½ oz) caster (superfine) sugar

pinch of ground cinnamon

4 large sheets of filo pastry

75 g (3 oz) butter, melted

icing (confectioners') sugar, for dusting

clotted cream, to serve

Mix together the apples, blackberries, sugar and cinnamon. Unwrap the filo pastry and cover with damp kitchen paper (paper towel) until ready to use it.

Working quickly, brush 1 sheet of pastry with the butter and arrange one-quarter of the apple mixture in a sausage shape along one short side, leaving a 2.5 cm (1 inch) space at each end. Fold the 2 long sides in over the mixture, then roll up the pastry to enclose it completely. Repeat to make 4 rolls in total.

Place the strudels on a baking sheet lined with baking paper. Bake in a preheated oven, 200°C (400°F), Gas Mark 6, for 15–20 minutes until crisp. Dust with icing sugar and serve with clotted cream.

# MINCEMEAT & APPLE STRUDEL

*Serves:* 6

*Prep time:* 10 minutes

*Cook time:* 20 minutes

2 small dessert apples, peeled, cored and diced

250 g (8 oz) mincemeat

50 g (2 oz) pecan nuts, chopped

4 sheets of filo pastry, about 48 x 25 cm (19 x 10 inches)

50 g (2 oz) unsalted butter, melted

icing (confectioners') sugar, for dusting

vanilla ice cream, to serve (optional)

Mix together the apples, mincemeat and pecans in a bowl.

Lay the first sheet of filo pastry on a clean tea towel (cloth kitchen towel) and brush with melted butter. Repeat with the remaining sheets of pastry, stacking them on top of each other.

Spread the mincemeat mixture over the pastry, leaving a 2.5 cm (1 inch) border. Fold in the short ends over the filling, then roll up like a Swiss roll, from one long edge, using the tea towel. Once rolled up, press the strudel gently together. Place on a baking sheet and brush with the remaining butter.

Bake in a preheated oven, 180°C (350°F), Gas Mark 4, for about 20 minutes, or until golden brown. Dust with icing sugar and serve with vanilla ice cream, if liked.

# Tarte Tatin with Mulled Pears

*Serves:* 6
*Prep time:* 30 minutes, plus cooling
*Cook time:* 45 minutes

- 50 g (2 oz) butter
- 150 g (5 oz) caster (superfine) sugar
- 200 ml (7 fl oz) red wine
- 1 cinnamon stick, broken in half
- 2 star anise
- 3 cloves
- 6 conference pears, about 750 g (1½ lb), halved, peeled and cored
- few drops of red food colouring (optional)
- 250 g (8 oz) ready-made puff pastry, defrosted if frozen

Melt the butter in a large frying pan (skillet), add the sugar, wine and spices and heat gently until the sugar has dissolved.

Add the pears to the red wine mix and simmer until the pears are almost tender (about 5 minutes), turning until evenly coloured. Scoop out of the pan and set aside.

Increase the heat and simmer the mixture for 5 minutes or until it is reduced and syrupy. Turn the heat off, stir in the food colouring, if using, then return the pears to the pan and coat in the syrup. Leave to cool for 15 minutes.

Roll out the pastry on a lightly floured surface, then trim to a 25 cm (10 inch) circle. Tip the pears, syrup and spices into a buttered metal pie dish, 20 cm (8 inches) in diameter and 5 cm (2 inches) deep. Lay the pastry on top, tucking it down the sides of the tin. Make 4 small steam vents in the top with a knife, then bake (unglazed) in a preheated oven, 200°C (400°F), Gas Mark 6, for 30 minutes until the pastry is risen, has shrunk from the sides of the tin and the juices are bubbling.

Leave to stand for 5 minutes. Loosen the edges with a knife, cover with a large serving plate, then invert the tin.

# Chocolate Filigree Torte

*Serves:* 10
*Prep time:* 30 minutes, plus cooling and chilling
*Cook time:* 20–25 minutes

3 eggs

75 g (3 oz) caster (superfine) sugar

50 g (2 oz) plain (all-purpose) flour

25 g (1 oz) cocoa powder

### FOR THE FILLING

2 teaspoons powdered gelatine

3 tablespoons cold water

200 g (7 oz) plain dark chocolate

500 g (1 lb) mascarpone, at room temperature

75 g (3 oz) caster (superfine) sugar

1 teaspoon vanilla extract

200 g (7 oz) Greek yogurt

4 tablespoons hot water

Whisk the eggs and sugar in a bowl over a pan of hot water until thickened. Remove from the heat and whisk for 2 minutes. Sift over the flour and cocoa powder, then fold in.

Grease and line a 23 cm (9 inch) springform or loose-based cake tin (cake pan), and pour in the mixture. Bake in a preheated oven, 190°C (375°F), Gas Mark 5, for 15 minutes until just firm. Cool on a wire rack.

Make the filling. Sprinkle the gelatine over the measurement water in a bowl and leave for 5 minutes. Cut the cake in half and put the bottom half back in the cake tin. Stand the bowl of gelatine in a pan of hot water until the gelatine has melted.

Melt 175 g (6 oz) of the chocolate over a pan of simmering water. Beat the mascarpone in a bowl with the sugar, vanilla extract, yogurt and measurement hot water. Whisking well, gradually pour the melted gelatine into the mascarpone mixture. Spoon half into a separate bowl and beat in the chocolate. Pour the chocolate mix onto the bottom half of the cake in the tin. Cover with the top sponge, then the remaining mascarpone (if this has started to set, beat in a little hot water). Level the surface and chill for several hours.

Lift the cake out of the tin, removing the nonstick baking paper, and transfer to a serving plate. Melt the remaining chocolate and drizzle it over the top. Chill until ready to serve.

# Tiny Treacle Tarts

*Makes:* 24
*Prep time:* 40 minutes, plus chilling
*Cook time:* 25 minutes

### FOR THE PÂTE SUCRÉE

175 g (6 oz) plain (all-purpose) flour, plus extra for dusting

40 g (1½ oz) icing (confectioners') sugar

100 g (3½ oz) butter, diced

2 egg yolks

### FOR THE FILLING

50 g (2 oz) butter

75 g (3 oz) light muscovado (brown) sugar

300 g (10 oz) golden syrup

grated rind of 1 lemon

2 tablespoons lemon juice

1 egg, beaten

50 g (2 oz) fresh breadcrumbs

### TO SERVE

whipped cream

ground cinnamon

Make the pâte sucrée. Add the flour, icing sugar and butter to a food processor or mixing bowl and mix until you have fine crumbs. Add the egg yolks and mix together until you have a soft ball. Wrap in clingfilm (plastic wrap) and chill for 15 minutes.

Roll the pastry out thinly on a lightly floured surface, then stamp out 24 × 6 cm (2½ inch) circles with a fluted biscuit (cookie) cutter and press into the buttered sections of 2 × 12-hole mini muffin tins. Re-knead and reroll the pastry trimmings as needed. Chill for 15 minutes.

Make the filling. Put the butter, golden sugar, syrup, lemon rind and juice in a small saucepan and cook over a low heat until the butter has just melted and the sugar dissolved. Take off the heat and leave to cool slightly.

Stir the beaten egg and breadcrumbs into the syrup mixture and beat until smooth. Spoon into the pastry cases.

Bake in a preheated oven, 180°C (350°F), Gas Mark 4, for 15–20 minutes. Leave to cool for 15 minutes, then loosen the tarts with a knife and remove from the tins. Transfer to a wire rack and leave to cool slightly. Serve warm with spoonfuls of whipped cream sprinkled with ground cinnamon.

# MINCEMEAT & APPLE PIES

*Makes:* 12

*Prep time:* 30 minutes

*Cook time:* 20 minutes

1 quantity pâte sucrée (see page 33) flavoured with 1 teaspoon ground cinnamon

125 g (4 oz) fruit mincemeat

75 g (3 oz) dried apricots, diced

1 dessert apple, peeled, cored and finely chopped

egg white, to glaze

icing (confectioners') sugar, for dusting

Reserve one-third of the pastry. Cut the rest in half, and roll one half out between 2 sheets of clingfilm (plastic wrap) until 5 mm (¼ inch) thick. Stamp out as many 6 cm (2½ inch) circles with a fluted biscuit (cookie) cutter as you can, peel off the clingfilm and press into the buttered sections of a 12-hole bun tin with your fingers dusted with rice flour. Roll out the other pastry half and repeat until you have 12 pie cases. Add the trimmings to the reserved pastry.

Mix the mincemeat with the apricots and apple, then spoon into the pie cases. Roll out the remaining pastry between clingfilm, then cut out 12 × 5 cm (2 inch) star shapes, add to the pie tops and brush with egg white.

Bake in a preheated oven, 190°C (375°F), Gas Mark 5, for about 20 minutes until golden. Leave to stand for 10 minutes, then loosen the edges with a small knife and lift out of the tin (the pies are more crumbly than those made with wheat flour, so take extra care). Leave to cool completely on a wire rack, then dust with icing sugar before serving.

# CARAMEL PEAR TARTE TATIN

*Serves:* 4–6

*Prep time:* 10 minutes

*Cook time:* 20 minutes

butter, for greasing

2 x 400 g (13 oz) cans pears in fruit juice, drained

5 tablespoons dulce de leche or thick caramel sauce

1 star anise

375 g (12 oz) readymade sweet shortcrust pastry, defrosted if frozen

plain (all-purpose) flour, for dusting

ice cream or cream, to serve

Line the base of a 23 cm (9 inch) loose-bottomed cake tin (cake pan) with baking paper and grease lightly.

Place the pears and dulce de leche or caramel sauce in a saucepan and heat over a gentle heat for 1–2 minutes, stirring occasionally, until the pears are well coated in the sauce. Arrange the pears, cut-side down, in the base of the prepared tin in a single layer, adding a star anise in the centre.

Roll out the pastry on a lightly floured work surface to a circle slightly larger than the tin and place over the pears, tucking the surplus down the side of the tin.

Bake in a preheated oven, 220°C (425°F), Gas Mark 7, for 20 minutes until the pastry is golden and cooked. Run a knife around the edge of the tart and carefully turn out onto a serving plate. Serve cut into wedges with ice cream or cream.

# Sweet Cherry Pies

*Makes:* 4
*Prep time:* 40 minutes, plus chilling
*Cook time:* 20–25 minutes

### FOR THE PASTRY

250 g (8 oz) plain (all-purpose) flour, plus extra for dusting

50 g (2 oz) caster (superfine) sugar, plus extra for sprinkling

pinch of salt

125 g (4 oz) butter, diced

2½–3 tablespoons cold water

milk or beaten egg, to glaze

### FOR THE FILLING

125 g (4 oz) caster (superfine) sugar

1 tablespoon cornflour (cornstarch)

½ teaspoon ground star anise or cinnamon

500 g (1 lb) frozen pitted black cherries, just defrosted, halved

custard, to serve

Make the pastry. Add the flour, sugar and salt to a large mixing bowl. Add the butter and rub it into the flour with your fingertips or use a freestanding electric mixer until the mixture resembles fine crumbs. Gradually mix in just enough water to enable the crumbs to be squeezed together to form a soft but not sticky dough. Knead very lightly until smooth, then wrap in clingfilm (plastic wrap) and chill for 15 minutes.

Mix the sugar, cornflour and star anise together, then add the cherries and toss together.

Roll out two-thirds of the pastry thinly on a lightly floured surface. Use to line 4 fluted loose-bottomed 10 cm (4 inch) tart tins, rerolling the pastry trimmings as needed.

Spoon the cherry mixture into the pastry cases, and brush the top edges with milk or beaten egg. Roll out the reserved pastry with any trimmings and cut 4 x 10 cm (4 inch) circles with a fluted biscuit (cookie) cutter.

Add the pie lids and press the pastry edges together to seal. Slash the tops with a knife, then brush the tops with milk or beaten egg and sprinkle with a little extra sugar.

Bake in a preheated oven, 180°C (350°F), Gas Mark 4, for 20–25 minutes until the pastry is golden. Leave to stand for 15 minutes, then loosen the edges of the pies and take out of the tin. Serve warm or cold with custard.

# Mile-High Chocolate Meringue Pie

*Serves:* 6
*Prep time:* 40 minutes, plus chilling
*Cook time:* 55–60 minutes

**FOR THE PASTRY**

- 110 g (3¾ oz) plain (all-purpose) flour, plus extra for dusting
- 15 g (½ oz) cocoa powder
- 40 g (1½ oz) caster (superfine) sugar
- 50 g (2 oz) butter, diced
- 4–5 teaspoons cold water

**FOR THE FILLING**

- 4 eggs, separated
- 175 g (6 oz) caster (superfine) sugar
- 3 tablespoons cocoa powder, sifted
- 1 tablespoon cornflour (cornstarch)
- 300 ml (½ pint) milk
- 1 teaspoon vanilla extract
- 40 g (1½ oz) dark chocolate, grated, plus extra to decorate

Make the pastry. Add the flour, cocoa powder, sugar and butter to a large bowl, then rub in with your fingertips or an electric mixer until you have fine crumbs. Mix in enough water to form a soft but not sticky dough. Roll out on a floured surface to fit a fluted loose-bottomed tart tin, 20 cm (8 inches) in diameter, 5 cm (2 inches) deep.

Line the tin with the pastry. Prick the base with a fork and chill for 15 minutes. Line with nonstick baking paper, add baking beans and blind bake the tart blind in a preheated oven, 190°C (375°F), Gas Mark 5 for 10 minutes. Remove the paper and beans and bake for a further 5 minutes.

Meanwhile, make the filling. Whisk the egg yolks and 50 g (2 oz) of the sugar, the cocoa powder and cornflour together in a large bowl. Pour the milk into a saucepan and bring to the boil. Gradually whisk the hot milk into the egg yolk mixture and then pour it back into the saucepan, whisking constantly until thick. Stir in the vanilla extract, then pour into the tart case.

Whisk the egg whites until stiff, then gradually whisk in the remaining sugar until it has all been added and the meringue is very thick, then fold in the grated chocolate. Spoon the meringue over the pie and shape into swirls. Bake at 180°C (350°F), Gas Mark 4, for 15 minutes until the meringue is golden. Cool before serving sprinkled with extra grated chocolate to decorate.

# Sweet Cranberry & Orange Pie

*Serves:* 6–8
*Prep time:* 30 minutes, plus cooling
*Cook time:* 35–40 minutes

500 g (1 lb) frozen cranberries

150 g (5 oz) caster (superfine) sugar

grated rind and juice of 1 orange

2 tablespoons water

1 tablespoon cornflour (cornstarch)

500 g (1 lb) ready-made puff pastry, defrosted if frozen

beaten egg, to glaze

**TO DECORATE**

100 g (3½ oz) icing (confectioners') sugar, sifted

grated rind and juice of ½ orange

Cook the cranberries in a saucepan with the sugar, orange rind and juice and the measurement water for 10 minutes, stirring occasionally until the cranberries are soft. Mix the cornflour to a paste with a little extra water, add to the cranberries and cook for a few minutes, stirring until thickened, then leave to cool.

Cut the pastry in half, roll out one half on a lightly floured surface and trim to a 20 × 25 cm (8 × 10 inch) rectangle, then transfer to a buttered baking sheet. Brush the beaten egg in a border around the edge of the rectangle, then pile the cranberry mixture in the middle.

Roll out the remaining pastry a little larger than the first and drape over the cranberries. Press the pastry edges together to seal well, then trim the top pastry layer to match the lower one. Knock up the edges of the pastry, then flute (see page 22).

Brush the top with beaten egg. Bake in a preheated oven, 200°C (400°F), Gas Mark 6, for 25–30 minutes until well risen and golden brown. Leave to cool for 30 minutes.

Mix the icing sugar with enough of the orange juice to make a smooth icing that just falls from a spoon, then drizzle randomly over the pie to decorate and sprinkle with the grated orange rind. Set aside for 20 minutes, or until the icing is set, then cut into slices to serve.

# Pumpkin Pie

*Serves:* 6–8
*Prep time:* 30 minutes
*Cook time:* 1–1¼ hours, plus cooling

- 500 g (1 lb) pumpkin or butternut squash, weighed after deseeding and peeling
- 3 eggs
- 100 g (3½ oz) light muscovado (brown) sugar
- 2 tablespoons plain (all-purpose) flour
- ½ teaspoon ground cinnamon
- ½ teaspoon ground ginger
- ¼ teaspoon grated nutmeg
- 200 ml (7 fl oz) milk, plus extra to glaze
- 450 g (14½ oz) chilled ready-made sweet shortcrust pastry
- icing (confectioners') sugar, for dusting
- whipped cream, to serve (optional)

Cut the pumpkin or butternut squash into cubes and cook in a covered steamer for 15–20 minutes, or until tender. Cool, then purée in a liquidizer or food processor.

Whisk the eggs, sugar, flour and spices together in a bowl until just mixed. Add the pumpkin purée, whisk together, then gradually mix in the milk. Set aside.

Roll out three-quarters of the pastry on a lightly floured surface until large enough to line a buttered 23 cm (9 inch) x 2.5 cm (1 inch) deep enamel pie dish. Lift the pastry over a rolling pin, drape into the dish and press over the base and sides. Trim off the excess and save the trimmings. Roll out the excess pastry thinly and cut tiny leaves, then mark veins. Brush the pastry rim with milk, then press on the leaves around the rim, reserving a few. Put the pie on a baking sheet.

Pour the pumpkin filling into the dish, add a few leaf decorations on top of the filling if liked, then brush these and the dish edges lightly with milk. Bake in a preheated oven, 190°C (375°F), Gas Mark 5, for 45–55 minutes until the filling is set and the pastry cooked through. Cover with foil after 20 minutes to stop the pastry edge from over-browning.

Serve dusted with a little icing sugar, and with whipped cream sprinkled with a little extra ground spice, if liked.

# SPICED PUMPKIN MERINGUE PIE

*Serves:* 6
*Prep time:* 30 minutes, plus chilling
*Cook time:* 1 hour 5 minutes

450 g (14½ oz) chilled ready-made sweet shortcrust pastry

500 g (1 lb) pumpkin, deseeded, peeled and diced

150 ml (¼ pint) double (heavy) cream

75 g (3 oz) light muscovado (brown) sugar

2 tablespoons clear honey

1 teaspoon ground ginger

1 teaspoon mixed spice

1 egg

3 egg yolks

vanilla ice cream, to serve (optional)

## FOR THE MERINGUE TOPPING

3 egg whites

50 g (2 oz) light muscovado (brown) sugar

50 g (2 oz) caster (superfine) sugar

½ teaspoon ground ginger

Roll the pastry out onto a lightly floured surface until large enough to line a buttered metal pie dish, 20 cm (8 inches) in diameter and 5 cm (2 inches) deep. Lift the pastry over a rolling pin, drape into the tin, then press over the base and sides. Trim the edges, then chill for 15 minutes.

Put the pumpkin in the top of a steamer, cover and cook for 10 minutes, or until tender. Mash with the cream, sugar, honey and spices, then beat in the whole egg and egg yolks. Pour into the pie case and level the surface. Bake in a preheated oven, 180°C (350°F), Gas Mark 4, for 40 minutes until set.

Make the meringue topping. Whisk the egg whites until you have stiff peaks, then gradually whisk in both sugars, a teaspoonful at a time, until all the sugar has been added. Add the ginger and whisk for 1–2 minutes more until very thick and glossy. Spoon over the hot pie and swirl the meringue with the back of a spoon. Bake for 15 minutes until lightly browned and the meringue is crisp.

Leave to cool for 30 minutes, then cut into wedges and serve warm with vanilla ice cream, if liked.

# Honeyed Pecan Pie

*Serves:* 8
*Prep time:* 30 minutes, plus chilling
*Cook time:* 40–45 minutes

1 quantity pâte sucrée (see page 33)

200 g (7 oz) clear honey

200 g (7 oz) light muscovado (brown) sugar

75 g (3 oz) butter, plus extra for greasing

¼ teaspoon ground cinnamon

1 teaspoon vanilla extract

3 eggs

150 g (5 oz) pecan nuts

vanilla ice cream, to serve

Roll the pastry out thinly on a lightly floured surface until a little larger than a buttered fluted loose-bottomed flan tin, 23 cm (9 inches) in diameter and 2.5 cm (1 inch) deep. Line the tin with the pastry. Trim off the excess pastry with scissors so that it stands a little above the top of the tin. Prick the base with a fork, then chill for 15 minutes.

Line the pastry case with nonstick baking paper add baking beans. Bake blind in a preheated oven, 190°C (375°F), Gas Mark 5, for 10 minutes. Remove the paper and beans and cook for a further 5 minutes until the case is crisp. Remove from the oven, and reduce the oven temperature to 180°C (350°F), Gas Mark 4.

Meanwhile, put the honey, sugar, butter and cinnamon into a saucepan and heat gently, stirring occasionally, until melted. Take off the heat and leave to cool slightly.

Beat the vanilla extract with the eggs in a small jug (pitcher), then gradually beat into the cooled honey mixture. Pour into the pastry case and arrange the nuts over the top.

Carefully transfer to the oven and bake for 25–30 minutes until the filling is set and the nuts have darkened. Check after 15 minutes and cover the top loosely with foil if the top seems to be browning too quickly.

Leave to cool in the tin for 30 minutes before serving with vanilla ice cream.

# DEEP DISH PUFF APPLE PIE

- 1 kg (2 lb) or about 5 cooking apples, peeled, quartered, cored and thickly sliced
- 100 g (3½ oz) caster (superfine) sugar, plus extra for sprinkling
- grated rind of 1 small orange
- ½ teaspoon ground mixed spice or ground cinnamon
- 3 whole cloves
- 400 g (13 oz) chilled ready-made puff pastry
- beaten egg, to glaze
- crème fraîche or extra-thick cream, to serve

Mix the sugar with the orange rind, mixed spice or cinnamon and cloves. Put the apples and sugar mixture in a bowl and toss to coat. Fill a 1.2 litre (2 pint) pie dish with the coated apples and set aside.

Roll the pastry out on a lightly floured surface until a little larger than the top of the dish. Cut 2 strips from a long edge, about 1 cm (½ inch) wide. Brush the dish rim with a little beaten egg, press the strips on top, then brush these with egg. Lift the remaining pastry over the dish and press the edges together well.

Trim off the excess pastry with a small knife, then crimp or flute the edges (see page 22). Reroll the trimmings and cut out small heart shapes or circles with a small biscuit (cookie) cutter. Brush the top of the pie with beaten egg, add the pastry shapes, then brush these with egg. Sprinkle with a little extra sugar.

Bake in a preheated oven, 200°C (400°F), Gas Mark 6, for 20–25 minutes until the pastry is well risen and golden. Serve warm with generous spoonfuls of crème fraîche or extra-thick cream.

# WHITE CHOCOLATE TORTE

*Serves:* 8
*Prep time:* 10 minutes, plus cooling
*Cook time:* 45 minutes

- 475 g (15 oz) white chocolate
- 125 g (4 oz) butter, plus extra for greasing
- 3 large eggs, separated
- 125 g (4 oz) golden caster (superfine) sugar
- 75 g (3 oz) wholemeal (wholewheat) self-raising flour, sifted
- 50 g (2 oz) ground almonds (almond meal)

Melt 225 g (7½ oz) of the chocolate with the butter in a bowl over a pan of simmering water. Reserve the rest of the chocolate for decoration.

Beat the egg yolks and sugar until pale, thick and foamy. Slowly whisk in the melted chocolate, then fold the flour and ground almonds into the mixture.

Whisk the egg whites in a large clean bowl until softly peaking. Beat a large spoonful of the egg whites into the chocolate mixture to loosen it slightly, then fold in the remainder using a large metal spoon.

Grease a 20 cm (8 inch) springform tin and line with a greaseproof cake liner or nonstick baking paper. Pour the mixture into the tin. Bake in a preheated oven, 180°C (350°F), Gas Mark 4, for 45 minutes, or until a skewer inserted into the centre comes out clean.

Cool in the tin for 10 minutes, then release and remove the sides of the tin and continue cooling. Grate half the reserved white chocolate and melt the rest in a bowl over a pan of simmering water. Spread the melted chocolate over the top of the cooled cake, then scatter over the gratings.

# Gingered Treacle Tart

*Serves:* 8
*Prep time:* 30 minutes
*Cook time:* 45–70 minutes

680 g (1 lb 6 oz) golden syrup
25 g (1 oz) butter
juice of 1 lemon
125 g (4 oz) fresh breadcrumbs
50 g (2 oz) glacé or stem ginger, drained and chopped
2 Braeburn apples, cored and coarsely grated

## FOR THE PASTRY

200 g (7 oz) plain (all-purpose) flour
100 g (3½ oz) butter, diced
2 tablespoons cold water
finely grated rindof 1 lemon
1 tablespoon milk
clotted cream or vanilla ice cream, to serve

Tip the golden syrup into a saucepan, add the butter and heat gently until melted. Remove from the heat and stir in the lemon juice, breadcrumbs, ginger and apples, then leave to cool.

Make the pastry. Put the flour, butter and lemon rind into a bowl and rub in the butter until the mixture resembles fine breadcrumbs. Add the measurement water and mix to a smooth dough, adding a little extra water if necessary. Knead lightly, roll out and use to line a 24 cm (9½ inch) loose-bottomed tart tin. Trim off the excess and reserve.

Pour the syrup mixture into the tart case. Roll out the pastry trimmings thinly, cut narrow strips and arrange in a lattice design, sticking the edges with a little milk. Then glaze all the strips with milk. Place the tart on a hot baking sheet. Bake in a preheated oven, 190°C (375°F), Gas Mark 5, for 40–50 minutes until golden and the filling has set. Cover the top loosely with foil after 30 minutes, if necessary, to prevent the tart burning.

When ready to serve, warm the tart in a preheated oven, 160°C (325°F), Gas Mark 3, for 15 minutes or serve cold with clotted cream or vanilla ice cream.

# Brandied Prune & Custard Tart

*Serves:* 8
*Prep time:* 30 minutes, plus standing and chilling
*Cook time:* 45–50 minutes

4 tablespoons brandy
250 g (8 oz) pitted prunes
150 ml (¼ pint) double (heavy) cream
150 ml (¼ pint) milk
1 vanilla pod, slit in half lengthways
1 quantity pâte sucrée (see page 33), chilled
4 eggs
50 g (2 oz) caster (superfine) sugar
icing (confectioners') sugar, for dusting

Warm the brandy in a saucepan, add the prunes, simmer gently for 3–4 minutes, then take off the heat. Pour the cream and milk into a second saucepan, add the vanilla pod and bring just to the boil, then take off the heat. Cover both pans and set aside for 2 hours.

Meanwhile, roll the pastry out on a lightly floured surface to fit a buttered 24 cm (9½ inch) fluted loose-bottomed tart tin, then press the pastry over the base and sides. Trim off the excess pastry with scissors so that it stands a little above the top of the tin. Prick the base with a fork and chill for 15 minutes.

Line the tart case with nonstick baking paper and add baking beans. Bake blind in a preheated oven, 190°C (375°F), Gas Mark 5 for 10 minutes. Remove the paper and baking beans and bake for a further 5 minutes. Remove from the oven and reduce the oven temperature to 180°C (350°F), Gas Mark 4.

Whisk the eggs and sugar together in a large bowl until creamy. Retrieve the vanilla pod, scrape out the seeds and add the seeds to the eggs, then whisk in the milk mixture.

Drain the prunes, adding the excess brandy to the milk mixture, then arrange in the tart case. Pour over the custard and bake for 25–30 minutes until the custard is pale golden and just set. Leave to cool, then remove from the tin and dust with icing sugar to serve.

# CHOCOLATE & GINGER TART

*Serves:* 6–8
*Prep time:* 15 minutes, plus cooling
*Cook time:* 15 minutes

200 g (7 oz) plain dark chocolate (85% cocoa solids), broken into small pieces
2 large eggs
50 g (2 oz) caster (superfine) sugar
2 pieces of stem ginger in syrup, finely chopped
100 ml (3½ fl oz) double (heavy) cream
20 cm (8 inch) shop-bought sweet pastry case (pie case)
cocoa powder, for dusting
vanilla ice cream or crème fraîche, to serve (optional)

Melt the chocolate in a heatproof bowl set over a saucepan of gently simmering water, stirring occasionally, then leave to cool slightly.

Place the eggs and sugar in a bowl and beat with a hand-held electric whisk until pale and fluffy. Whisk in the melted chocolate until well combined, then stir in the stem ginger and cream.

Place the pastry case on a baking sheet. Pour in the chocolate mixture and spread the top level. Bake in a preheated oven, 160°C (325°F), Gas Mark 3, for 10–12 minutes, or until just set. The mixture should be slightly wobbly in the centre, as it will continue to set on cooling.

Dust with cocoa powder. Serve warm or cold with vanilla ice cream or crème fraîche, if liked.

# CINNAMON TARTS

*Makes:* 12
*Prep time:* 5 minutes, plus cooling
*Cook time:* 25 minutes

375 g (12 oz) sheet ready-rolled puff pastry
pinch of ground nutmeg
½ teaspoon ground cinnamon
2 tablespoons caster (superfine) sugar

### FOR THE FILLING

3 egg yolks
50 g (2 oz) caster (superfine) sugar
2 tablespoons cornflour (cornstarch)
1 teaspoon vanilla extract
finely grated rind of ¼ lemon
300 ml (½ pint) double (heavy) cream

Unroll the pastry and sprinkle over the nutmeg, cinnamon and sugar. Then tightly reroll and cut it into 12 x 1.5 cm (¾ inch) slices. Roll each slice into a small round on a lightly floured surface. Turn a 12-hole muffin tin upside down, gently press each round over the top of a muffin mould and chill in the freezer for 5 minutes.

Bake in a preheated oven, 220°C (425°F), Gas Mark 7, for 5 minutes, then place the pastry cases on a baking tray (baking sheet).

Make the filling. Put the egg yolks, sugar, cornflour, vanilla extract and lemon rind in a bowl and whisk until smooth. Add the cream and whisk again, then cook in a saucepan for 5 minutes, stirring frequently, until the mixture is thick. Spoon the custard into the pastry cases. Turn up the oven to 230°C (450°F), Gas Mark 8, and bake for 12–15 minutes until caramelized and set.

# Pecan, Maple Syrup & Chocolate Tart

*Serves:* 8
*Prep time:* 20 minutes, plus chilling and cooling
*Cook time:* 1 hour 10 minutes

125 g (4 oz) unsalted butter, at room temperature
125 g (4 oz) light soft brown sugar
2 eggs, beaten
4 tablespoons plain (all-purpose) flour
pinch of salt
175 ml (6 fl oz) maple syrup
175 g (6 oz) pecan nuts, toasted
100 g (3½ oz) pine nuts, lightly toasted
50 g (2 oz) plain dark chocolate, chopped

## FOR THE PASTRY

200 g (7 oz) plain (all-purpose) flour, sifted, plus extra for dusting
¼ teaspoon salt
100 g (3½ oz) unsalted butter, diced
1 egg, lightly beaten
2–3 teaspoons cold water

Make the pastry. Add the flour, salt and butter to a bowl, then rub the butter in with your fingertips or an electric mixer until you have fine crumbs. Add the egg and measurement water and continue mixing until the pastry just starts to come together. Transfer to a lightly floured surface and knead gently. Wrap the dough in clingfilm (plastic wrap) and chill for 30 minutes.

Roll out the dough thinly on a lightly floured surface and use it to line a 23 cm (9 inch) square flan tin. Prick the base with a fork and chill for 20 minutes. Line the tart case with nonstick baking paper and add baking beans. Bake blind in a preheated oven, 190°C (375°F), Gas Mark 5, for 15 minutes.

Remove the paper and baking beans and bake for a further 5–10 minutes until crisp and golden. Leave to cool. Reduce the oven temperature to 180°C (350°F), Gas Mark 4.

Cream the butter and sugar until pale and light, then gradually beat in the eggs, adding the flour and salt as you go until evenly combined. Stir in the maple syrup (the mixture may appear to curdle at this stage), nuts and chocolate and spoon the mixture into the pastry case.

Bake for 40–45 minutes until golden and just firm in the centre. Remove from the oven and leave to cool. Serve warm with ice cream.

# TOFFEE APPLE TARTS

*Makes:* 12
*Prep time:* 40 minutes, plus chilling
*Cook time:* 20 minutes

1 quantity pâte sucrée (see page 45), chilled

2 teaspoons cornflour (cornstarch)

2 tablespoons water

750 g (1½ lb) dessert apples, peeled, cored and diced

100 g (3½ oz) light muscovado (brown) sugar

25 g (1 oz) butter

**FOR THE TOPPING**

250 ml (8 fl oz) double (heavy) cream

3 tablespoons light muscovado (brown) sugar

Roll the pastry out thinly on a lightly floured surface, then stamp out 12 × 10 cm (4 inch) circles with a fluted biscuit (cookie) cutter and press into a buttered 12-section muffin tin, rerolling the pastry trimmings as needed. Prick the bases 2–3 times, then chill for 15 minutes.

Line the tart cases with nonstick baking paper and add baking beans. Bake the tarts blind in a preheated oven, 190°C (375°F), Gas Mark 5 for 5 minutes. Remove the paper and baking beans and cook for a further 4–5 minutes until pale golden. Remove from the oven, and reduce the oven temperature to 180°C (350°F), Gas Mark 4.

Meanwhile, mix the cornflour and the measurement water to a paste in a saucepan, add the apples, sugar and cook for 10 minutes, stirring from time to time, until the butter and apples are soft. Leave to cool for 15 minutes, then loosen the tarts and remove from the tin.

Spoon the apples into the tart cases. Whip the cream to form soft swirls. Fold in 2 tablespoons sugar, spoon over the tarts and sprinkle with the remaining sugar. Serve cold.

# Honey, Grape & Cinnamon Tartlets

*Makes:* 16
*Prep time:* 25 minutes, plus cooling
*Cook time:* 10 minutes

- 100 g (3½ oz) seedless red grapes, peeled and halved
- 100 g (3½ oz) seedless white grapes, peeled and halved
- 3 tablespoons dessert wine or grape juice
- 25 g (1 oz) unsalted butter, melted
- ½ teaspoon ground cinnamon
- 3 sheets of filo pastry
- plain (all-purpose) flour, for dusting
- 100 ml (3½ fl oz) double (heavy) cream
- 100 ml (3½ fl oz) Greek yogurt
- 2 tablespoons clear honey, plus extra to drizzle

Place 16 mini silicone muffin cases on a baking sheet.

Put the grapes in a bowl with the dessert wine or grape juice.

Mix the melted butter and the cinnamon. Unfold the pastry sheets on a lightly floured surface, then put one in front of you – covering the others with clingfilm (plastic wrap). Cut into 6.5 cm (2¾ inch) squares. Brush the squares lightly with the spiced butter. Cut out more squares from the other 2 sheets and position over the first, adjusting the positions so the points are evenly staggered. Press into the cases and brush with a little more butter.

Bake in a preheated oven, 190°C (375°F), Gas Mark 5, for 10 minutes until golden. Transfer to a wire rack to cool.

Beat the cream with the yogurt and honey until just holding its shape. Drain the grapes over the cream and beat the juice into the cream. Spoon the cream mixture into the pastry cases and pile the grapes on top. Serve drizzled with extra honey.

# MUFFINS, CUPCAKES & LOAVES

# Spiced Ginger Cupcakes

*Makes:* 12
*Prep time:* 5 minutes, plus cooling
*Cook time:* 15 minutes

150 g (5 oz) unsalted butter, softened

125 g (4 oz) soft dark brown sugar

1 tablespoon clear honey

3 large eggs, lightly beaten

150 g (5 oz) plain (all-purpose) flour

2 teaspoons baking powder

1 teaspoon ground ginger

pinch of ground cloves

### FOR THE ICING

50 g (2 oz) icing (confectioners') sugar, sifted

15 g (½ oz) stem ginger in syrup, drained and cut into thin matchsticks

1 tablespoon stem ginger syrup (from the jar)

½ teaspoon water

Line a 12-hole cupcake tray with paper cases. Place the butter, sugar, honey and eggs in a large bowl, then sift in the flour, baking powder, ground ginger and cloves. Beat together with a hand-held electric whisk until the mixture is pale and creamy.

Spoon the mixture into the prepared tray. Bake in a preheated oven, 200°C (400°F), Gas Mark 6, for 12–15 minutes until risen and firm to the touch.

Meanwhile, make the icing. Mix together all the ingredients in a small bowl until runny and smooth.

Remove the cupcakes from the oven, then transfer to a wire rack and drizzle over the ginger icing. Serve warm or cold.

# CHILLI CHOCOLATE CHIP MUFFINS

*Makes:* 8

*Prep time:* 20 minutes

*Cook time:* 20 minutes

200 g (7 oz) self-raising flour

50 g (2 oz) cocoa powder

1 teaspoon baking powder

150 g (5 oz) soft light brown sugar

1 egg

250 ml (8 fl oz) milk

50 g (2 oz) butter, melted

125 g (4 oz) chilli chocolate, chopped, or plain dark chocolate, chopped, and a pinch of chilli powder

75 g (3 oz) pecan nuts, toasted and roughly ground

spray olive oil, for greasing

Cut a 15 cm (6 inch) square from baking paper and use it as a template to cut 7 more. Open out flat and set aside.

Sift the flour, cocoa powder and baking powder into a bowl and stir in the sugar. Beat together the egg, milk and melted butter in a jug (pitcher). Add to the dry ingredients and stir together using a large metal spoon until just combined. Fold in the chocolate or chocolate and chilli powder and pecan nuts.

Spray each square of baking parchment with oil and press each piece into the hole of a muffin tray. Spoon the mixture into the lined holes. Bake in a preheated oven, 200°C (400°F), Gas Mark 6, for 20 minutes until risen and golden. Transfer to a wire rack to cool slightly, then serve warm.

# BANOFEE CHOCOLATE MUFFINS

*Makes:* 6

*Prep time:* 10 minutes, plus cooling

*Cook time:* 18-22 minutes

225 g (7½ oz) self-raising flour, sifted

2 tablespoons cocoa powder, sifted

100 g (3½ oz) caster (superfine) sugar

100 g (3½ oz) dark chocolate chips

2 eggs

2 small ripe bananas, mashed

50 ml (2 fl oz) vegetable oil

125 g (4 oz) natural (plain) yogurt

warmed toffee sauce, to serve

Line a 12-hole cupcake tray with paper cases. In a bowl, mix the flour, cocoa powder, sugar and 75 g (3 oz) of the chocolate chips together.

Combine the eggs, bananas, oil and yogurt in a bowl, then pour the wet ingredients into the dry and mix until only just combined. Divide the mixture evenly between the cases and scatter over the remaining chocolate chips.

Bake in a preheated oven, 180°C (350°F), Gas Mark 4, for 18–22 minutes until risen and firm to the touch. Cool slightly on a wire rack and serve warm, drizzled with warm toffee sauce.

# CHOCOLATE SEA SALT CUPCAKES

VG

*Makes:* 12 small cupcakes
*Prep time:* 10–15 minutes, plus cooling
*Cook time:* 15–20 minutes

100 g (3½ oz) self-raising flour

100 g (3½ oz) light brown sugar

25 g (1 oz) cocoa powder

pinch of salt

75 ml (3 fl oz) hot coffee or boiling water

60 ml (2½ fl oz) dairy-free milk

60 ml (2½ fl oz) flavourless oil

1 teaspoon vanilla extract (optional)

## FOR THE ICING

50 g (2 oz) 70% cocoa dark chocolate

50 g (2 oz) icing (confectioners') sugar

2 tablespoons dairy-free milk

sea salt flakes, to sprinkle

Line a 12-hole cupcake tin or bun tin with small cake cases, or just use squares of nonstick baking paper.

In a large bowl, whisk together the flour, sugar, cocoa powder and salt until no lumps remain.

Add the coffee or boiling water, milk, oil and vanilla extract, if using, and whisk well until you have a smooth batter.

Spoon 1–2 tablespoons of batter into each of the cake cases. Bake in a preheated oven, 180°C (350°F), Gas Mark 4, for 14–16 minutes until firm and springy to the touch and a skewer inserted into the centre comes out clean.

Remove the cakes from the tin and leave to cool on a wire rack.

Make the icing. Melt the chocolate in a microwave in 30 second bursts or in a heatproof bowl over a pan of just-boiled water (don't let the bowl touch the water). Whisk the melted chocolate with the icing sugar and milk until you have a thick but spreadable icing. Top each cake with 1 teaspoon of icing and a pinch of sea salt flakes.

Store in an airtight container for up to 4 days.

# MARSALA RAISIN COFFEE MUFFINS

*Makes:* 16
*Prep time:* 15 minutes, plus soaking
*Cook time:* 12 minutes

50 g (2 oz) raisins

4 tablespoons marsala

1 teaspoon instant espresso coffee powder

2 teaspoons boiling water

125 g (4 oz) self-raising flour

½ teaspoon baking powder

65 g (2½ oz) golden caster (superfine) sugar

125 g (4 oz) natural (plain) yogurt

1 egg, beaten

2 tablespoons vegetable oil

## FOR THE ICING

½ teaspoon espresso coffee powder

1½ teaspoons hot water

40 g (1½ oz) icing (confectioners') sugar, sifted

Place 16 mini silicone muffin cases on a baking sheet.

Put the raisins and marsala in a small saucepan and heat until hot but not boiling. Pour into a bowl and leave to stand for 2 hours until the raisins have plumped up.

Mix the coffee powder with the boiling water. Sift the flour and baking powder into a bowl. Stir in the sugar.

Mix together the yogurt, egg, oil and coffee mixture and stir in the raisins and any unabsorbed liquid. Add to the dry ingredients. Using a large metal spoon, stir the ingredients together until only just combined. Divide the mixture between the cases.

Bake in a preheated oven, 200°C (400°F), Gas Mark 6, for about 12 minutes until risen and firm. Leave in the cases for 2 minutes, then transfer to a wire rack to cool.

Make the icing. Mix the espresso coffee powder in a small bowl with the hot water until blended. Beat in the icing sugar and drizzle over the muffins.

# CAPPUCCINO CUPCAKES

*Makes:* 12
*Prep time:* 30 minutes
*Cook time:* 12–14 minutes

3 teaspoons instant coffee
2 teaspoons boiling water
175 g (6 oz) soft margarine
175 g (6 oz) light muscovado sugar
175 g (6 oz) self-raisingflour
½ teaspoon baking powder
3 eggs

### TO DECORATE

300 ml (½ pint) double (heavy) cream
75 g (3 oz) dark or white
chocolate curls

Dissolve the coffee in the boiling water.

Beat the remaining cake ingredients in a mixing bowl until smooth. Stir in the dissolved coffee. Divide the mixture among the greased and base-lined sections of a 12-hole deep muffin tin and level the surfaces.

Bake in a preheated oven, 180°C (350°F), Gas Mark 4, for 12–14 minutes until well risen and the cakes spring back when gently pressed with a fingertip.

Leave to cool in the tin for 5 minutes then loosen the edges, turn out onto a wire rack and peel off the lining paper. Leave to cool completely.

Turn each cake the right way up then slice in half horizontally. Whip the cream until softly peaking then use to sandwich the cakes together in pairs and spread the remainder on the tops. Sprinkle with chocolate curls.

# APPLE & CINNAMON MUFFINS

*Makes:* 6
*Prep time:* 10 minutes, plus cooling
*Cook time:* 20-22 minutes

butter, for greasing
200 g (7 oz) wholemeal (whole-wheat) flour
50 g (2 oz) fine oatmeal
1 teaspoon baking powder
1 teaspoon bicarbonate of soda (baking soda)
½ teaspoon ground cinnamon
100 g (3½ oz) soft light brown sugar
pinch of salt
200 g (7 oz) apple, apple and apricot, or apple and blueberry purée
150 ml (¼ pint) buttermilk
3 tablespoons groundnut oil
2 large eggs, lightly beaten

Lightly grease a 6-hole nonstick extra-large muffin tray.

In a large bowl, mix all the dry ingredients together.

Beat the remaining ingredients together in a large jug (pitcher) and pour into the dry mixture. Use a large metal spoon to stir until only just combined, then spoon the batter into the prepared tray. Bake in a preheated oven, 180°C (350°F), Gas Mark 4, for 20–22 minutes until risen, firm and golden. Remove from the oven and transfer the muffins to a wire rack to cool slightly. Serve warm.

# SPICED SWEET POTATO CUPCAKES

*Makes:* 9
*Prep time:* 25 minutes, plus cooling
*Cook time:* 35 minutes

125 g (4 oz) sweet potato
10 cardamom pods
50 g (2 oz) lightly salted butter
6 tablespoons clear honey
2 eggs, beaten
100 g (3½ oz) self-raising flour
½ teaspoon baking powder
3 tablespoons flaked (slivered) almonds, toasted
50 g (2 oz) golden icing (confectioners') sugar
2 teaspoons lemon juice

Line 9 holes of a 12-hole cupcake tray with paper cases. Scrub the sweet potato and cut into chunks. Cook in a saucepan of boiling water for 10 minutes, or until tender. Drain well and return to the pan. Mash until smooth and leave to cool.

Crush the cardamom pods using a pestle and mortar or in a small bowl using the end of a rolling pin, to release the seeds. Discard the husks and crush the seeds as finely as possible.

Melt the butter in a small saucepan with the honey. Transfer to a bowl and leave to cool slightly. Beat in the sweet potato and cardamom, then the eggs, flour and baking powder.

Divide the mixture between the cases and scatter with the flaked almonds.

Bake in a preheated oven, 180°C (350°F), Gas Mark 4, for 20 minutes, or until risen and just firm. Transfer to a wire rack to cool.

Beat the icing sugar with the lemon juice in a bowl to make a smooth, thin glacé icing. Drizzle thin lines of icing back and forth across the cakes.

*Makes:* 12
*Prep time:* 25 minutes
*Cook time:* 20–25 minutes

# LEMON & CARDAMOM CUPCAKES

- 1 tablespoon cardamom pods
- finely grated rind of 2 lemons
- 150 g (5 oz) caster (superfine) sugar
- 150 g (5 oz) lightly salted butter, softened
- 2 eggs
- 175 g (6 oz) self-raising flour
- 1 tablespoon lemon juice
- chopped lemon jellies, to decorate

### FOR THE ICING

- 175 g (6 oz) icing (confectioners') sugar, sifted
- 2 tablespoons lemon juice
- yellow food colouring (optional)

Line a 12-hole cupcake tray with paper cases. Crush the cardamom pods using a pestle and mortar or in a small bowl using the end of a rolling pin, to release the seeds. Discard the husks and crush the seeds as finely as possible.

Reserve ¼ teaspoon of the crushed seeds for the decoration and put the remaining seeds in a food processor with the lemon rind and sugar. Process lightly until the sugar is almost powdered. Add the butter, eggs, flour and lemon juice. Blend until soft and creamy, scraping the mixture down from the side of the bowl.

Divide the mixture between cases. Bake in a preheated oven, 180°C (350°F), Gas Mark 4, for 20–25 minutes until just firm to the touch. Transfer to a wire rack to cool.

Make the icing. Beat together the icing sugar and lemon juice in a bowl until combined. Add a dash of yellow food colouring, if using, and a few drops of water or extra lemon juice to make a smooth, spreadable icing. Spread over the cupcakes, then decorate with lemon jellies and sprinkle with the reserved cardamom.

# MAPLE & PECAN MUFFINS

*Makes:* 8
*Prep time:* 10 minutes
*Cook time:* 20–25 minutes

300 g (10 oz) self-raising flour
1 teaspoon baking powder
125 g (4 oz) soft brown sugar
1 egg
50 ml (2 fl oz) maple syrup
250 ml (8 fl oz) milk
50 g (2 oz) unsalted butter, melted
125 g (4 oz) white chocolate, finely chopped
75 g (3 oz) pecan nuts, coarsely chopped

### TO DECORATE

chopped pecans
chopped white chocolate

Line 8 holes of a 12-hole muffin tray with paper cases. Sift the flour and baking powder into a mixing bowl and stir in the sugar. Beat together the egg, maple syrup, milk and melted butter, then beat into the dry ingredients until mixed. Fold in the chocolate and pecans.

Divide the mixture between the cases and top with some extra chopped nuts and chocolate.

Bake in a preheated oven, 200°C (400°F), Gas Mark 6, for 20–25 minutes until risen and golden. Transfer to a wire rack to cool.

# CINNAMON SUGAR MUFFINS

*Makes:* 12
*Prep time:* 10 minutes
*Cook time:* 18-20 minutes

200 g (7 oz) plain (all-purpose) flour
2 teaspoons baking powder
1½ teaspoons ground cinnamon
50 g (2 oz) bran
100 g (3½ oz) caster (superfine) sugar
3 tablespoons demerara sugar
2 large eggs
1 ripe banana, mashed
50 g (2 oz) butter, melted
175 ml (6 fl oz) buttermilk

Line a 12-hole muffin tray with paper cases. Sift the flour, baking powder and ½ teaspoon of the cinnamon into a large bowl. Stir in the bran and caster sugar. In a separate bowl, combine the remaining cinnamon with the demerara sugar and set aside.

Put the eggs, banana, butter and buttermilk in a jug (pitcher) or bowl and beat well. Pour over the dry ingredients and mix until only just combined.

Spoon the batter into the prepared tray and sprinkle with the cinnamon sugar. Bake in a preheated oven, 180°C (350°F), Gas Mark 4, for 18–20 minutes until risen and firm to the touch.

Transfer the muffins to a wire rack to cool slightly, and serve warm.

# TRIPLE CHOCOLATE CUPCAKES

*Makes:* 12

*Prep time:* 30 minutes, plus cooling and setting

*Cook time:* 40 minutes

150 g (5 oz) butter or margarine

150 g (5 oz) caster (superfine) sugar

175 g (6 oz) self-raising flour

3 eggs

1 teaspoon vanilla extract

## TO DECORATE

100 g (3½ oz) white chocolate, chopped

100 g (3½ oz) milk chocolate, chopped

100 g (3½ oz) plain chocolate, chopped

40 g (1½ oz) unsalted butter

Whisk the butter or margarine, sugar, flour, eggs and vanilla extract in a mixing bowl until light and creamy.

Line a 12-hole cupcake tray with paper cases. Divide the mixture evenly between the cases. Bake in a preheated oven, 180°C (350°F), Gas Mark 4, for 18–20 minutes until risen and just firm to the touch. Transfer to a wire rack to cool.

Meanwhile, put the white, milk and plain chocolate in separate microwave-proof or heatproof bowls and add one-third of the butter to each. Melt all the chocolate, either one at a time in a microwave or by setting each bowl over a saucepan of very gently simmering water, stirring occasionally until smooth.

Spread the melted white chocolate over 4 of the cakes using a small palette knife.

Put 2 tablespoons of the melted milk and plain chocolate in separate piping bags, fitted with writing nozzles. Spread the milk chocolate over 4 more of the cakes and pipe lines of plain chocolate over the milk chocolate.

Spread the plain chocolate over the remaining 4 cakes and scribble with lines of piped milk chocolate. Leave to set.

# MARBLED COFFEE CUPCAKES

*Makes:* 12
*Prep time:* **15 minutes**
*Cook time:* **20 minutes**

125 g (4 oz) lightly salted butter, softened
125 g (4 oz) caster (superfine) sugar, plus 2 teaspoons to sprinkle
2 eggs
150 g (5 oz) self-raising flour
½ teaspoon baking powder
2 teaspoons espresso coffee powder
1 teaspoon boiling water
50 g (2 oz) flaked (slivered) almonds, toasted
¼ teaspoon ground cinnamon

Line a 12-hole cupcake tray with paper cases. Put the butter, the 125 g (4 oz) sugar, eggs, flour and baking powder in a bowl and beat with a hand-held electric whisk for about 1 minute until light and creamy.

Spoon half the mixture into a separate bowl. Blend the coffee powder with the boiling water and stir into half the mixture. Using a teaspoon, fill the cases with both mixtures, then draw a knife in a circular motion through each cupcake to partially mix the mixtures together to create a marbled effect.

Scatter the flaked almonds over the cakes. Mix the remaining 2 teaspoons of sugar with the cinnamon and sprinkle over the cakes.

Bake in a preheated oven, 180°C (350°F), Gas Mark 4, for 20 minutes, or until risen and just firm to the touch. Transfer to a wire rack to cool.

# MINCEMEAT MUFFINS

*Makes:* 10
*Prep time:* **10 minutes**
*Cook time:* **18–20 minutes**

300 g (10 oz) self-raising flour
1 teaspoon baking powder
1 teaspoon ground mixed spice
100 g (3½ oz) soft light brown sugar
175 g (6 oz) mincemeat
2 eggs, lightly beaten
100 g (3½ oz) unsalted butter, melted
175 ml (6 fl oz) buttermilk
1 tablespoon milk
2 teaspoons demerara sugar

Line 10 holes of a 12-hole muffin tray with paper cases. Mix the flour, baking powder, mixed spice and brown sugar in a large bowl. In a separate bowl, mix together the mincemeat, egg, melted butter, buttermilk and milk. Add the wet ingredients to the dry and mix briefly until just combined.

Divide the mixture between the paper cases, then sprinkle the tops evenly with the demerara sugar.

Bake in a preheated oven, 200°C (400°F), Gas Mark 6, for 18–20 minutes, or until risen and golden. Cool in the tray for 10 minutes, then transfer to a wire rack. Serve warm or cold.

# Pumpkin Spice Cupcakes

*Makes:* 12
*Prep time:* 30 minutes, plus cooling
*Cook time:* 10–15 minutes

100 g (3½ oz) lightly salted butter, softened

100 g (3½ oz) caster (superfine) sugar

a few drops of vanilla extract

2 eggs

100 g (3½ oz) self-raising flour

1 teaspoon ground ginger

1 teaspoon mixed spice

### TO DECORATE

125 g (4 oz) red ready-to-roll icing

125 g (4 oz) yellow ready-to-roll icing

125 g (4 oz) green ready-to-roll icing

125 g (4 oz) black ready-to-roll icing

black icing pen (optional)

Line a 12-hole bun tray with paper cases. Put the butter, sugar and vanilla extract in a bowl and beat with a wooden spoon until light and creamy. Add the eggs and beat the mixture again, then sift in the flour, ground ginger and mixed spice and stir in. Divide the mixture between the cases.

Bake in a preheated oven, 180°C (350°F), Gas Mark 4, for 10–15 minutes, or until risen and firm to the touch. Transfer to a wire rack to cool.

Knead together the red and the yellow icing to make orange icing. Roll a little piece of the green icing into a ball, then flatten into a round and gently push onto the top of a cake. Roll a larger piece of the orange icing into a ball. Place on top of the green 'pumpkin patch' base. Roll a tiny piece of green icing into a stalk and push onto the top of the orange pumpkin. Use the black icing to make eyes and a crooked smile. Alternatively, draw the features onto the pumpkin head with a black icing pen.

# Marzipan Cupcakes

*Makes:* 12
*Prep time:* 30 minutes, plus cooling and soaking
*Cook time:* 30 minutes

125 g (4 oz) lightly salted butter, softened, plus extra for greasing

50 g (2 oz) light muscovado (brown) sugar

1 piece of stem ginger from a jar, finely chopped

2 eggs

150 g (5 oz) self-raising flour

½ teaspoon baking powder

½ teaspoon freshly grated nutmeg

200 g (7 oz) luxury mixed dried fruit, soaked in 3 tablespoons brandy or orange-flavoured liqueur for 1 hour

325 g (11 oz) white almond paste

icing (confectioners') sugar, for dusting

2 tablespoons ginger syrup

Line a 12-hole cupcake tray with paper cases. Put the butter, sugar, ginger, eggs, flour, baking powder and nutmeg in a bowl and beat with a hand-held electric whisk for about 1 minute until smooth and creamy. Stir in the fruit and any liquid until evenly mixed.

Roll 100 g (3½ oz) of the almond paste into a log shape, about 6 cm (2½ inches) long, and cut into 12 slices. Divide half the mixture between the cases and level with the back of a teaspoon. Place a paste slice over each. Cover with the remaining mixture.

Bake in a preheated oven, 180°C (350°F), Gas Mark 4, for about 25 minutes until just firm to the touch. Transfer to a wire rack to cool.

Roll out the remaining paste thinly on a work surface lightly dusted with icing sugar. Cut out 12 rounds with a 5 cm (2 inch) cookie cutter. Brush the cakes with the ginger syrup and cover each with a paste round. Flatten a small piece of leftover paste into a thin ribbon and roll up to make a rose. Position on the cake centre. Repeat for the remaining cakes. Put on a baking sheet and heat under a moderate grill (broiler), watching closely, until lightly toasted.

# STOLLEN SLICE

*Makes:* 15 slices
*Prep time:* 30 minutes, plus proving
*Cook time:* 25 minutes

- 40 g (1½ oz) salted butter, plus extra for greasing
- 175 g (6 oz) strong white bread flour, plus extra for dusting
- 1½ teaspoons fast-action dried yeast
- ½ teaspoon ground mixed spice
- 25 g (1 oz) caster (superfine) sugar
- 100 ml (3½ fl oz) warm milk
- 75 g (3 oz) sultanas
- 25 g (1 oz) almonds, chopped
- 25 g (1 oz) candied peel, chopped
- 150 g (5 oz) marzipan
- icing (confectioners') sugar, for dusting

Grease the base and long sides of a 1 kg (2 lb) loaf tin (loaf pan). Put the flour, yeast, mixed spice and sugar in a bowl. Melt 25 g (1 oz) of the butter, mix with the milk and add to the bowl. Mix with a round-bladed knife to make a soft but not sticky dough. Turn out onto a lightly floured surface and knead for 10 minutes until smooth and elastic. (Alternatively, use a freestanding mixer with a dough hook and knead for 5 minutes.) Place in a lightly oiled bowl, cover with clingfilm (plastic wrap) and leave to rise in a warm place for about 1½ hours, or until doubled in size.

Turn the dough out onto a floured surface and knead in the sultanas, almonds and candied peel. Cover loosely with a tea towel (cloth kitchen towel) and leave to rest for 10 minutes. Roll out the dough on a floured surface to a 25 x 20 cm (10 x 8 inch) rectangle. Roll the marzipan under the palms of your hands to form a log shape about 23 cm (9 inches) long and flatten to about 5 mm (¼ inch) thick. Lay the marzipan down the length of the dough, slightly to one side, and fold the rest of the dough over it. Transfer to the tin and press down gently.

Cover loosely with oiled clingfilm and leave to rise in a warm place for about 30 minutes until slightly risen. Remove the clingfilm. Bake in a preheated oven, 220°C (425°F), Gas Mark 7, for 25 minutes until risen and golden. Leave for 5 minutes, then turn out of the tin, place on a wire rack, cover with a sheet of foil and place a couple of food cans or pack of icing sugar on top to keep the stollen compact, while cooling on the wire rack. Melt the remaining butter and brush over the stollen. Dust generously with icing sugar.

# PEANUT CUPCAKES

*Makes:* 16
*Prep time:* 20 minutes, plus cooling
*Cook time:* 15 minutes

65 g (2½ oz) lightly salted butter, softened
65 g (2½ oz) light muscovado (brown) sugar
65 g (2½ oz) self-raising flour
1 egg
50 g (1½ oz) salted peanuts, finely chopped, plus extra to decorate

## FOR THE FROSTING

50 g (2 oz) lightly salted butter
100 g (3½ oz) light muscovado (brown) sugar
3 tablespoons milk
75 g (3 oz) golden icing (confectioners') sugar

Place 16 mini silicone cupcake cases on a baking sheet.

Put the butter, sugar, flour and egg in a bowl and beat with a hand-held electric whisk until light and creamy. Stir in the nuts. Divide the mixture between the cases.

Bake in a preheated oven, 180°C (350°F), Gas Mark 4, for 10–12 minutes, or until risen and just firm. Leave in the cases for 2 minutes, then transfer to a wire rack to cool.

Make the frosting. Heat the butter, sugar and milk in a saucepan until the sugar dissolves. Bring to the boil and boil for 1 minute until the mixture turns slightly syrupy. Remove from the heat and pour into a bowl. Sift the icing sugar into the bowl and beat until the mixture is smooth and fudge-like.

Spread the frosting over the tops of the cakes, and scatter with chopped peanuts.

# CHOCOLATE RIPPLE LOAF

*Makes:* 1 large loaf
*Prep time:* 15 minutes, plus cooling
*Cook time:* 1½ hours

200 g (7 oz) plain dark chocolate
200 g (7 oz) butter, plus extra for greasing
1 teaspoon ground mixed spice
175 g (6 oz) golden caster (superfine) sugar
3 eggs
2 teaspoons vanilla extract
225 g (7½ oz) self-raising flour
½ teaspoon baking powder
100 g (3½ oz) plain dark chocolate, chopped

Melt the chocolate in a bowl over a pan of simmering water, ensuring the bowl does not touch the water, and stir in 25 g (1 oz) of the butter and the mixed spice.

Place the remaining butter, sugar, eggs and vanilla extract in a bowl. Sift the flour and baking powder into the bowl and beat until light and fluffy.

Grease the base and long sides of a 1 kg (2 lb) loaf tin (loaf pan). Spoon one-quarter of the mixture into the tin. Spread one-third of the chocolate mixture over the cake mixture. Repeat the layering of the cake mixture and chocolate mixture, finishing with a layer of cake mixture. Sprinkle with the chopped chocolate.

Bake in a preheated oven, 180°C (350°F), Gas Mark 4, for 1¼ hours, or until risen and a skewer inserted into the centre comes out clean. Leave in the tin for 10 minutes, then transfer to a wire rack to cool.

# MINCE PIE CUPCAKES

*Makes:* 12
*Prep time:* 20 minutes, plus cooling
*Cook time:* 20–25 minutes

125 g (4 oz) lightly salted butter, softened

25 g (1 oz) dark muscovado (brown) sugar

2 eggs

150 g (5 oz) self-raising flour

½ teaspoon baking powder

1 teaspoon ground mixed spice

1 tablespoon milk

300 g (10 oz) luxury mincemeat

## FOR THE TOPPING

300 ml (½ pint) double (heavy) cream

4 tablespoons sherry

2 tablespoons icing (confectioners') sugar

edible pink and silver balls, to decorate

Line a 12-hole cupcake tray with silver or gold foil cases. Put the butter, sugar, eggs, flour, baking powder, mixed spice and milk in a bowl and beat with a hand-held electric whisk for about 1 minute until light and creamy. Add the mincemeat and stir in until evenly mixed. Divide the mixture between the foil cases.

Bake in a preheated oven, 180°C (350°F), Gas Mark 4, for 20–25 minutes, or until risen and just firm to the touch. Transfer to a wire rack to cool.

Make the topping. Put the cream, sherry and icing sugar in a bowl and whip until the mixture only just holds its shape. Pile the cream over the cakes and scatter with pink and silver balls to decorate.

# Carrot & Walnut Cupcakes

*Makes:* 12

*Prep time:* 20 minutes, plus cooling

*Cook time:* 25 minutes

150 g (5 oz) lightly salted butter, softened

150 g (5 oz) light muscovado (brown) sugar

3 eggs

150 g (5 oz) self-raising flour

½ teaspoon baking powder

1 teaspoon ground mixed spice

75 g (3 oz) ground walnuts

finely grated rind of 1 orange

150 g (5 oz) carrots, grated

50 g (2 oz) sultanas

### FOR THE FROSTING

125 g (4 oz) full-fat cream cheese

275 g (9 oz) icing (confectioners') sugar

1 tablespoon lemon juice

chopped walnuts, to decorate

Line a 12-hole cupcake tray with paper cases. Put the butter, sugar, eggs, flour, baking powder, mixed spice, ground walnuts and orange rind in a bowl and beat with a hand-held electric whisk for about 1 minute until light and creamy.

Stir in the grated carrots and sultanas until evenly mixed. Divide the mixture between the cases.

Bake in a preheated oven, 180°C (350°F), Gas Mark 4, for 25 minutes, or until risen and just firm to the touch. Leave in the tray for 5 minutes, then transfer to a wire rack to cool.

Make the frosting. Beat the cream cheese in a bowl with a wooden spoon until smooth and creamy. Beat in the icing sugar and lemon juice. Spread over the tops of the cakes using a small palette knife and scatter with the chopped walnuts to decorate.

# Pomegranate & Ginger Slice

*Cuts into:* 20
*Prep time:* 25 minutes
*Cook time:* 50 minutes

200 g (7 oz) plain (all-purpose) flour

1 teaspoon bicarbonate of soda (baking soda)

100 ml (3½ fl oz) milk

1 egg

100 g (3½ oz) dark muscovado (brown) sugar

125 g (4 oz) black treacle (molasses)

75 g (3 oz) unsalted butter

3 pieces of stem ginger in syrup, chopped

## FOR THE TOPPING

300 ml (½ pint) pomegranate juice

2 tablespoons clear honey

1 pomegranate

Sift the flour and bicarbonate of soda into a bowl. Beat together the milk and egg in a jug (pitcher). Put the sugar, treacle and butter in a saucepan and heat gently until the butter melts and the sugar dissolves. Remove from the heat and add to the milk mixture with the stem ginger.

Add to the dry ingredients and stir together using a large metal spoon until well combined.

Spoon the mixture into 2 greased and lined 1 kg (2 lb) loaf tins (loaf pans) and level the surface. Bake in a preheated oven, 160°C (325°F), Gas Mark 3, for 30 minutes, or until just firm to the touch and a skewer inserted into the centre comes out clean. Leave to cool in the tins, then loosen at the ends and transfer to a wire rack. Peel off the lining paper.

Make the topping. Pour the pomegranate juice into a saucepan and bring to the boil, then boil for about 15 minutes until reduced to a thick and syrupy consistency. Stir in the honey. Halve the pomegranate and push the halves inside out to release the fleshy seeds, discarding any white membrane. Scatter the seeds over the top of the cakes. Drizzle with the syrup and cut into small squares to serve.

# CINNAMON BUTTER FANCIES

*Makes:* 12
*Prep time:* 10 minutes, plus cooling
*Cook time:* 8 minutes

50 g (2 oz) rolled oats
25 g (1 oz) demerara sugar
50 g (2 oz) chopped mixed nuts
25 g (1 oz) unsalted butter
23 cm (9 inch) shop-bought square, plain sponge cake
1 teaspoon ground cinnamon
25 g (1 oz) dried blueberries

### FOR THE ICING

75 g (3 oz) unsalted butter, softened
125 g (4 oz) icing (confectioners') sugar, sifted
1 teaspoon ground cinnamon
2 teaspoons coffee essence

Mix together the oats, sugar and nuts in a large bowl. Heat the butter in a large, nonstick frying pan (skillet), add the oat mixture and toast over a medium–low heat for 6–8 minutes, stirring frequently until golden. Tip onto a plate and leave to cool.

Meanwhile, make the icing. Place all the ingredients in a large bowl and beat together with a hand-held electric whisk until light and fluffy. Spread the icing over the sponge cake, then cut the cake into 12 squares.

Stir the cinnamon and blueberries into the toasted oats, then sprinkle generously over the iced squares.

# PEANUT BUTTER & CHOCOLATE MUFFINS

*Makes:* 12
*Prep time:* 10 minutes
*Cook time:* 20 minutes

25 g (1 oz) unsalted butter
100 g (3½ oz) crunchy peanut butter
150 g (5 oz) plain (all-purpose) flour
1½ teaspoons baking powder
pinch of salt
75 g (3 oz) soft light brown sugar
1 large egg
125 ml (4 fl oz) buttermilk
50 g (2 oz) milk chocolate chunks or chips

Line a 12-hole mini muffin tin with paper cases. Place the butter and peanut butter in a small saucepan over a low heat and warm until just melted. Stir gently, then set aside.

Meanwhile, sift the flour, baking powder and salt into a large bowl, then stir in the sugar. Whisk together the egg, buttermilk and melted butters in a jug (pitcher). Pour into the dry ingredients and stir until just combined.

Spoon the mixture into the cases, then scatter over the chocolate chunks or chips.

Bake in a preheated oven, 200°C (400°F), Gas Mark 6, for 10–15 minutes until risen and golden. Serve warm.

# Jamaican Ginger Cake

*Makes:* 1 large loaf
*Prep time:* 30 minutes
*Cook time:* 50–60 minutes

- 150 g (5 oz) butter, plus extra for greasing
- 150 g (5 oz) golden syrup
- 150 g (5 oz) black treacle (molasses)
- 150 g (5 oz) plain (all-purpose) flour
- 150 g (5 oz) wholemeal (whole-wheat) bread flour
- 4 teaspoons ground ginger
- 1 teaspoon ground mixed spice
- 1 teaspoon bicarbonate of soda (baking soda)
- 2 eggs, beaten
- 4 tablespoons milk

### FOR THE TOPPING

- 1 tablespoon apricot jam (jelly)
- 125 g (4 oz) exotic dried fruit, cut into strips
- 1 piece of stem ginger, drained and sliced

Grease a 1 kg (2 lb) loaf tin (loaf pan), its base and 2 long sides also lined with oiled greaseproof paper (wax paper). Put the butter, golden syrup and treacle in a saucepan and heat gently, stirring occasionally, until the butter has melted. Remove from the heat and cool for 5 minutes.

Mix all the dry ingredients together in a large mixing bowl. Gradually stir in the syrup mixture, then the eggs and milk and beat well until smooth.

Pour into the prepared loaf tin. Bake in a preheated oven, 160°C (325°F), Gas Mark 3, for 50–60 minutes until well risen, the top has cracked and a skewer inserted into the centre comes out clean. Leave to cool in the tin for 10 minutes, then loosen the edges and lift out of the tin using the lining paper. Transfer to a wire rack, peel off the lining paper and leave to cool.

Spread the top of the cake with the apricot jam, then decorate with strips of exotic dried fruit and the ginger.

# Chocolate Iced Fancies

*Makes:* 16
*Prep time:* 45 minutes, plus cooling
*Cook time:* 25 minutes

100 g (3½ oz) lightly salted butter, softened, plus extra for greasing
125 g (4 oz) plain dark chocolate, chopped
125 g (4 oz) light muscovado (brown) sugar
2 eggs
50 g (2 oz) self-raising flour
25 g (1 oz) cocoa powder
50 g (2 oz) ground almonds (almond meal)
5 tablespoons shop-bought chocolate hazelnut spread

**FOR THE ICING**

200 g (7 oz) plain dark chocolate, chopped
2 tablespoons golden syrup
15 g (½ oz) lightly salted butter
50 g (2 oz) milk chocolate, chopped

Grease and line a 15 cm (6 inch) square tin with nonstick baking paper. Grease the paper.

Melt the chocolate in a heatproof bowl set over a saucepan of gently simmering water, ensuring the bowl does not touch the water. Stir gently and set aside. Beat together the butter and sugar in a bowl until pale and creamy. Gradually beat in the eggs, adding a little flour to prevent the mixture curdling. Stir in the melted chocolate.

Sift the flour and cocoa powder over the bowl. Add the ground almonds and stir in gently.

Pour into the prepared tin and level the surface. Bake in a preheated oven, 160°C (325°F), Gas Mark 3, for about 20 minutes until risen and just firm to the touch. Transfer to a wire rack to cool.

Cut the cake into 16 squares and, using a palette knife, spread a little mound of chocolate hazelnut spread on the top of each one.

Make the icing. Melt the plain dark chocolate with the golden syrup and butter until smooth and glossy. Separately melt the milk chocolate. Spoon a little of the plain chocolate mixture over each cake and spread around the sides with a palette knife. Using a teaspoon, drizzle lines of milk chocolate over each cake.

# Sticky Toffee & Date Loaf

*Makes:* 1 large loaf

*Prep time:* 20 minutes, plus cooling

*Cook time:* 1 hour 10 minutes–1 hour 15 minutes

250 g (8 oz) pitted dates, roughly chopped

300 g (10 oz) self-raising flour

1 teaspoon baking powder

1 large egg, beaten

175 ml (6 fl oz) milk

50 g (2 oz) unsalted butter, melted, plus extra for greasing

¼ teaspoon salt

1½ teaspoons ground mixed spice

icing (confectioners') sugar, for dusting

### FOR THE TOFFEE SAUCE

300 ml (½ pint) double (heavy) cream

125 g (4 oz) light brown sugar

50 g (2 oz) butter

Put the dates in a small saucepan with 5 tablespoons of water. Cover and cook gently for about 5 minutes until the dates have softened and the water has been absorbed. Leave to cool.

Meanwhile, make the toffee sauce. Heat half the cream in a small, heavy-bottomed pan with the sugar and butter until the sugar dissolves. Bring to the boil, then let the sauce bubble for about 5 minutes until a rich, dark caramel. Stir in the remaining cream and set aside.

Put the flour and baking powder in a mixing bowl. Add half of the toffee sauce, the egg, milk, butter, salt and mixed spice, and mix together. Stir in the dates, then spoon into a greased 1 kg (2 lb) loaf tin (loaf pan), its base and 2 long sides also lined with greased paper.

Bake in the centre of a preheated oven, 160°C (325°F), Gas Mark 3, for 1 hour 10 minutes–1¼ hours until well risen, the top has cracked and a skewer inserted into the centre comes out clean. Leave to cool for 10 minutes, then loosen the edges, turn out onto a wire rack and peel off the lining paper. Leave to cool completely, then dust with icing sugar.

Serve freshly baked or lightly toasted with the remaining sauce spooned over. If the sauce has become very thick on cooling, it can be heated gently to soften.

# Cidered Apple & Fig Loaf

*Makes:* 1 large loaf
*Prep time:* 20 minutes, plus soaking
*Cook time:* 1 hour–1 hour 10 minutes

300 ml (½ pint) dry cider
1 large cooking apple (about 300 g /10 oz), peeled, cored and chopped
175 g (6 oz) dried figs, chopped
150 g (5 oz) caster (superfine) sugar
300 g (10 oz) self-raising flour
2 eggs, beaten
1 tablespoon sunflower seeds
1 tablespoon pumpkin seeds
butter, to serve

Pour the cider into a saucepan, add the apple and figs and bring to the boil. Simmer for 3–5 minutes until the apples are just tender but still firm. Remove the pan from the heat and leave to soak for 4 hours.

Mix the sugar, flour and eggs into the soaked fruit and stir well.

Spoon into a greased 1 kg (2 lb) loaf tin (loaf pan), its base and 2 long sides also lined with greased baking paper, and spread the surface level. Sprinkle with the seeds.

Bake in the centre of a preheated oven, 160°C (325°F), Gas Mark 3, for 1 hour–1 hour 10 minutes until well risen, the top has slightly cracked and a skewer inserted into the centre comes out clean.

Leave to cool in the tin for 10 minutes, then loosen the edges and lift out of the tin using the baking paper. Transfer to a wire rack, peel off the lining paper and leave to cool completely. Serve cut into 10 slices and spread with a little butter. Store in an airtight container for up to 1 week.

# STICKY SULTANA & BRAN SLICE

*Makes:* 1 large loaf

*Prep time:* 10 minutes, plus standing

*Cook time:* 45 minutes

200 g (7 oz) sultanas

125 g (4 oz) demerara sugar, plus extra for sprinkling

2 tablespoons black treacle (molasses)

100 g (3½ oz) shredded bran or bran flake cereal

1 teaspoon ground mixed spice

300 ml (½ pint) milk

150 g (5 oz) self-raising flour

Mix together the sultanas, sugar, treacle, bran, mixed spice and milk in a bowl. Leave to stand for 20 minutes to allow the bran to soften. Stir in the flour.

Tip the mixture into a greased and lined 1 kg (2 lb) loaf tin (loaf pan) and level the surface. Bake in a preheated oven, 160°C (325°F), Gas Mark 3, for about 45 minutes, or until risen, firm to the touch and a skewer inserted into the centre comes out clean. Loosen the cake at the ends and transfer to a wire rack. Peel off the lining paper and leave to cool. Cut into slices and spread with a little butter to serve.

# BANANA, DATE & WALNUT LOAF

*Makes:* 1 large loaf

*Prep time:* 25 minutes

*Cook time:* 1 hour 10 minutes–1¼ hours

4 bananas, peeled and mashed

1 tablespoon lemon juice

300 g (10 oz) self-raising flour

1 teaspoon baking powder

125 g (4 oz) caster (superfine) sugar

125 g (4 oz) butter, melted

2 eggs, beaten

175 g (6 oz) dates, chopped

50 g (2 oz) walnut pieces

## TO DECORATE

walnut halves

banana chips

Mash the bananas with the lemon juice.

Put the flour, baking powder and sugar in a mixing bowl. Add the bananas, butter and eggs and mix together. Stir in the dates and walnut pieces then spoon into a greased 1 kg (2 lb) loaf tin (loaf pan), its base and 2 long sides also lined with oiled greaseproof paper (wax paper). Level the surface and decorate with walnut halves and banana chips.

Bake in the centre of a preheated oven, 160°C (325°F), Gas Mark 3, for 1 hour 10 minutes–1¼ hours until well risen and a skewer inserted into the centre comes out clean. Leave to cool for 10 minutes then loosen the edges, turn out on to a wire rack and peel off the lining paper. Leave to cool completely, then slice.

# Glazed Pear & Cinnamon Loaf

*Makes:* 1 large loaf
*Prep time:* 10 minutes, plus soaking
*Cook time:* 1 hour 10 minutes – 1 hour 20 minutes

- 100 g (3½ oz) dried pears, chopped
- 100 g (3½ oz) sultanas
- 400 ml (14 fl oz) strong, hot tea
- 375 g (12 oz) self-raising flour
- 1 teaspoon baking powder
- 75 g (3 oz) light muscovado (brown) sugar
- 1 egg, beaten
- 25 g (1 oz) unsalted butter, softened, plus extra for greasing
- ¼ teaspoon salt
- 2 teaspoons ground cinnamon
- icing (confectioners') sugar, for dusting

Place the pears and sultanas in a bowl with the hot tea and leave to soak for 1 hour.

Put the flour, baking powder and sugar in a mixing bowl. Add the egg, butter, salt and cinnamon and mix together. Stir in the sultanas with the pears and liquid, then spoon into a greased 1 kg (2 lb) loaf tin (loaf pan), its base and 2 long sides also lined with greased paper.

Bake in the centre of a preheated oven, 160°C (325°F), Gas Mark 3, for 1 hour 10 minutes–1¼ hours until well risen, the top has cracked and a skewer inserted into the centre comes out clean. Leave to cool for 10 minutes then loosen the edges, turn out on to a wire rack and peel off the lining paper. Leave to cool completely, then dust with icing sugar.

Serve freshly baked or toasted and buttered.

# Pear, Cardamom & Sultana Cake

*Makes:* 1 large loaf
*Prep time:* 20 minutes
*Cook time:* 1¼–1½ hours

- 125 g (4 oz) unsalted butter, at room temperature
- 125 g (4 oz) light soft brown sugar
- 2 eggs, lightly beaten
- 250 g (8 oz) self-raising flour
- 1 teaspoon ground cardamom
- 4 tablespoons milk
- 500 g (1 lb) pears, peeled, cored and thinly sliced
- 125 g (4 oz) sultanas
- 1 tablespoon clear honey

Beat the butter and sugar together in a mixing bowl until pale and creamy. Gradually beat in the eggs, a little at a time, until incorporated. Sift the flour and ground cardamom together and fold them into the creamed mixture with the milk.

Reserve about one-third of the pear slices and roughly chop the rest. Fold the chopped pears into the creamed mixture with the sultanas. Spoon the mixture into a greased 1 kg (2 lb) loaf tin (loaf pan), its base and 2 long sides also lined with greased paper. Spread the surface level.

Arrange the reserved pear slices along the centre of the cake, pressing them in gently. Bake in a preheated oven, 160°C (325°F), Gas Mark 3, for 1¼–1½ hours, or until a skewer inserted into the centre comes out clean.

Remove the cake from the oven. Leave to cool in the tin for 10 minutes, then loosen the edges and lift out of the tin using the lining paper. Transfer to a wire rack, peel off the lining paper and leave to cool completely. Drizzle with the honey.

# Maple Syrup & Macadamia Madeleines

*Makes:* 18
*Prep time:* 20 minutes, plus cooling
*Cook time:* 9 minutes

- 2 large eggs
- 100 g (3½ oz) caster (superfine) sugar
- 2 tablespoons maple syrup, plus extra to serve (optional)
- pinch of salt
- 125 g (4 oz) plain (all-purpose) flour, plus extra for dusting
- ½ teaspoon baking powder
- 50 g (2 oz) macadamia nuts, very finely chopped
- 125 g (4 oz) unsalted butter, melted and cooled, plus extra for greasing

Place the eggs, sugar, maple syrup and salt in a large bowl and beat with a hand-held electric whisk until pale and thick and doubled in volume. Sift in the flour and baking powder, then add the macadamia nuts and melted butter and fold in until combined. Cover and chill for at least 10 minutes. (This helps the traditional 'bump' to form in the centre of each madeleine.)

Meanwhile, grease 18 holes of 2 x 12-hole madeleine trays with melted butter, then dust lightly with flour, tapping the tin to remove any excess.

Gently stir the madeleine mixture, then spoon into the prepared trays until each hole is about three-quarters full. Bake in a preheated oven, 220°C (425°F), Gas Mark 7, for 3 minutes, then reduce the temperature to 200°C (400°F), Gas Mark 6, and bake for a further 4–6 minutes until risen and golden.

Transfer to a wire rack to cool slightly, then serve warm, drizzled with extra warmed maple syrup, if liked.

# Chocolate Orange Madeleines

*Makes:* 12
*Prep time:* 15 minutes, plus cooling
*Cook time:* 15 minutes

- 75 g (3 oz) butter, melted and cooled, plus extra for greasing
- 75 g (3 oz) self-raising flour, plus extra for dusting
- 2 large eggs
- 1 teaspoon orange extract
- 1 teaspoon finely grated orange rind
- 75 g (3 oz) caster (superfine) sugar
- pinch of salt
- 100 g (3½ oz) plain dark or milk chocolate, broken into small pieces

Lightly brush a 12-hole madeleine tray with melted butter and dust lightly with flour.

Place the eggs, orange extract, orange rind, sugar and salt in a large bowl and beat with a hand-held electric hand whisk until pale and thick and the whisk leaves a trail when lifted above the mixture. Sift in the flour, then add the melted butter and fold gently until combined.

Spoon into the prepared tray until each hole is about three-quarters full. Bake in a preheated oven, 200°C (400°F), Gas Mark 6, for 8–10 minutes until risen and golden.

Meanwhile, melt the chocolate in a heatproof bowl set over a saucepan of gently simmering water, ensuring the bowl does not touch the water. Stir gently and set aside.

Remove the madeleines from the oven and transfer to a wire rack. Once cool to the touch, spread some melted chocolate over each cake. Leave to set in a cool place for a few minutes before serving.

# Chocolate Raspberry Friands

*Makes:* 10
*Prep time:* 20 minutes
*Cook time:* 20 minutes

- 100 g (3½ oz) lightly salted butter
- 75 g (3 oz) plain chocolate, at room temperature
- 100 g (3½ oz) ground almonds (almond meal)
- 125 g (4 oz) golden caster (superfine) sugar
- 40 g (1½ oz) plain (all-purpose) flour
- 3 egg whites
- 150 g (5 oz) fresh raspberries
- icing (confectioners') sugar, for dusting (optional)

Line 10 holes of a 12-hole cupcake tray with paper cases. Melt the butter in a small saucepan and leave to cool. Coarsely grate the chocolate – if the chocolate is brittle and difficult to grate, try softening it in a microwave for a few seconds first, but take care not to overheat and melt it.

Mix together the ground almonds, 75 g (3 oz) of the sugar and the flour in a large bowl. Stir in the melted butter and grated chocolate until just combined.

Whisk the egg whites in a thoroughly clean bowl until peaking. Gradually whisk in the remaining sugar. Using a large metal spoon, fold half the egg whites into the chocolate mixture to lighten it, then fold in the remainder until evenly combined.

Divide the mixture evenly between the cases and scatter the raspberries on top.

Bake in a preheated oven, 200°C (400°F), Gas Mark 6, for 15 minutes, or until golden and just firm to the touch. Transfer to a wire rack to cool. Serve dusted with icing sugar, if liked.

# BISCUITS, BROWNIES & TRAYBAKES

# Rich Chocolate Macarons

*Makes:* 12

*Prep time:* 20 minutes, plus standing and cooling

*Cook time:* 20 minutes

50 g (2 oz) icing (confectioners') sugar

50 g (2 oz) ground almonds (almond meal)

4 tablespoons cocoa powder

2 egg whites

100 g (3½ oz) caster (superfine) sugar

**FOR THE FILLING**

5 tablespoons double (heavy) cream

100 g (3½ oz) plain dark chocolate, chopped

Line 2 baking sheets with nonstick baking paper. Put the icing sugar, ground almonds and cocoa powder in a food processor and blend to a very fine consistency.

Put the egg whites in a thoroughly clean bowl and whisk until peaking. Gradually whisk in the sugar, a tablespoonful at a time and whisking well after each addition, until thick and very glossy. Add the almond mixture to the bowl and use a metal spoon to stir the ingredients together to combine.

Place the mixture in a piping bag fitted with a 1 cm (½ inch) plain nozzle, and pipe 24 x 3 cm (1¼ inch) rounds onto the baking sheets. Tap the baking sheet firmly to smooth the surfaces of the macarons slightly, then leave to stand for 30 minutes. Bake in a preheated oven, 160°C (325°F), Gas Mark 3, for about 15 minutes, or until the surfaces feel crisp. Leave to cool before carefully peeling away the paper.

Make the filling. Heat the cream in a small saucepan until bubbling up around the edges but not boiling. Remove from the heat and stir in the chocolate. Leave the chocolate to melt, stirring frequently, until smooth. Once the chocolate is cool and thickened enough to hold its shape, use to sandwich the macarons together in pairs. Keep in a cool place until ready to serve.

# Chocolate Peanut Butter Whoopie Pies

***Makes:*** 15
***Prep time:*** 20 minutes, plus cooling
***Cook time:*** 20 minutes

300 g (10 oz) self-raising flour

2 teaspoons baking soda

50 g (2 oz) cocoa powder

175 g (6 oz) light brown sugar

1 egg, beaten

75 ml (3 fl oz) vegetable oil

150 ml (¼ pint) buttermilk

75 ml (3 fl oz) boiling water

100 g (3½ oz) plain dark chocolate

### FOR THE FILLING

125 g (4 oz) cream cheese

100 g (3½ oz) smooth peanut butter

200 g (7 oz) icing (confectioners') sugar

Line two large baking sheets with nonstick baking paper. Place the flour, baking soda, cocoa power and sugar in a large bowl. Mix the egg, oil and buttermilk with the boiling water and stir into the dry ingredients until well mixed.

Spoon 30 tablespoonfuls of the mixture onto the prepared sheets, making sure they are spaced well apart. Bake in a preheated oven, 180°C (350°F), Gas Mark 4, for 10–12 minutes, or until just firm. Leave to cool.

Make the filling. Beat together the cream cheese and peanut butter until smooth. Sift in the icing sugar and beat until well combined. Pipe or spoon the icing over 15 halves, then sandwich the remaining 15 on top.

Melt the chocolate in a small bowl set over a pan of simmering water, making sure the water does not touch the bottom of the bowl. Spoon over the whoopie pies before serving.

# Walnut & White Chocolate Cookies

*Makes:* about 25
*Prep time:* 15 minutes, plus cooling
*Cook time:* 12–15 minutes

1 egg
150 g (5 oz) soft light brown sugar
2 tablespoons caster (superfine) sugar
1 teaspoon vanilla extract
125 ml (4 fl oz) vegetable oil
65 g (2½ oz) plain (all-purpose) flour
3 tablespoons self-raising flour
¼ teaspoon ground cinnamon
25 g (1 oz) shredded coconut
175 g (6 oz) walnuts, toasted and chopped
125 g (4 oz) white chocolate chips

Line 2 baking sheets with nonstick baking paper. In a bowl, beat the egg and sugars together until light and creamy. Stir in the vanilla extract and oil. Sift in the flours and cinnamon, then add the coconut, walnuts and chocolate and mix well.

Form rounded tablespoonfuls of the mixture into 25 balls and place on the prepared baking sheets, pressing the mixture together with your fingertips if it is crumbly.

Bake in a preheated oven, 180°C (350°F), Gas Mark 4, for 12–15 minutes, or until golden. Leave to cool slightly on the sheets, then transfer to a wire rack to cool completely.

# Chocolate Chip Cookies

VG

*Makes:* 8 large cookies

*Prep time:* 25 minutes, plus chilling

*Cook time:* 10 minutes, plus cooling

- 150 g (5 oz) soft light brown sugar
- 2 tablespoons cornflour (cornstarch)
- 75 g (3 oz) coconut oil, melted
- 50 ml (2 fl oz) dairy-free milk
- 1 teaspoon vanilla extract (optional)
- ¼ teaspoon bicarbonate of soda (baking soda)
- ¼ teaspoon baking powder
- ½ teaspoon fine sea salt
- 200 g (7 oz) plain (all-purpose) flour
- 125 g (4 oz) 70% cocoa dark chocolate, roughly chopped

Line a baking sheet with nonstick baking paper.

In a large bowl, whisk together the sugar, cornflour and coconut oil until just combined. Add the milk and vanilla extract, if using, and whisk for 1 minute until noticeably thickened.

Sprinkle over the bicarbonate of soda, baking powder, salt and flour and whisk again to combine. Add the chocolate and use your hand to fully incorporate it.

Using 2 tablespoons, divide the dough into 8 portions and place on the prepared tray. Don't worry about trying to get them perfectly round; the melted coconut oil will mean they're too soft to shape yet.

Refrigerate for 15 minutes, then roll each portion between your hands to get a uniform ball. Try to leave some of the larger chunks of chocolate on top of the cookie, to get those signature gooey pools. Leave 4 cookies in the refrigerator on a plate lined with baking paper.

Bake the other 4 cookies on the tray in a preheated oven, 180°C (350°F), Gas Mark 4, for 10 minutes, leaving plenty of room between each one as they will spread.

Leave to cool on the tray for 2 minutes before transferring to a wire rack to cool fully, while you bake the remaining cookies in the same way.

# Triple Chocolate Biscotti

***Makes:*** **about 28**
***Prep time:*** **35 minutes, plus cooling**
***Cook time:*** **45 minutes**

- 50 g (2 oz) lightly salted butter, softened
- 50 g (2 oz) caster (superfine) sugar
- 175 g (6 oz) self-raising flour, plus extra for dusting
- 1 teaspoon baking powder
- ½ teaspoon ground coriander
- finely grated rind of 1 orange, plus 1 tablespoon of the juice
- 50 g (2 oz) polenta
- 1 egg, lightly beaten
- 100 g (3½ oz) unblanched almonds, roughly chopped
- 75 g (3 oz) milk chocolate chips
- 150 g (5 oz) plain dark chocolate, broken into pieces
- 50 g (2 oz) white chocolate, broken into pieces

Beat the butter and sugar until creamy. Add the flour, baking powder, coriander, orange rind and juice, polenta and egg and mix to form a firm dough. Knead in the almonds. Turn the dough out onto a lightly floured surface and gently work in the chocolate chips. Divide the mixture in half and shape each piece into a log about 23 cm (9 inches) long.

Place on a greased baking sheet, spaced well apart, and flatten slightly. Bake in a preheated oven, 160°C (325°F), Gas Mark 3, for 30 minutes, or until risen and just firm. Remove from the oven and cool on the baking sheet for 15 minutes. Transfer to a board and, using a serrated knife, cut into 1 cm (½ inch) thick slices.

Arrange on the baking sheet, cut-sides down, and bake for 15 minutes until crisp. Transfer to a wire rack and leave to cool.

Melt the plain dark and white chocolate in 2 separate heatproof bowls over pans of simmering water. Line a tray or clean baking sheet with nonstick baking paper. Dip about one-third of each biscotti in the plain dark chocolate, letting the excess fall back into the bowl. Place each biscotti on the baking paper.

Drizzle thin lines of melted white chocolate over the plain dark chocolate to decorate. Leave in a cool place to set for about 1 hour.

# PEANUT BUTTER COOKIES

*Makes:* 32

*Prep time:* 10 minutes

*Cook time:* 12 minutes

125 g (4 oz) unsalted butter, softened, plus extra for greasing

150 g (5 oz) soft brown sugar

125 g (4 oz) crunchy peanut butter

1 egg, lightly beaten

150 g (5 oz) plain (all-purpose) flour

½ teaspoon baking powder

125 g (4 oz) unsalted peanuts

Beat together the butter and sugar in a bowl or food processor until pale and creamy. Add the peanut butter, egg, flour and baking powder and stir together until combined. Stir in the peanuts.

Drop large teaspoonfuls of the mixture onto 3 large, lightly greased baking sheets, leaving 5 cm (2 inch) gaps between each one for them to spread during cooking. Flatten the mounds slightly with a fork.

Bake in a preheated oven, 190°C (375°F), Gas Mark 5, for 12 minutes until golden around the edges. Leave to cool on the baking sheets for 2 minutes, then transfer to a wire rack to cool completely.

# CLOVE & CARDAMOM COOKIES

*Makes:* 30–40

*Prep time:* 15 minutes, plus cooling

*Cook time:* 16 minutes

175 g (6 oz) unsalted butter, softened

200 g (7 oz) soft dark brown sugar

1 large egg, lightly beaten

½ teaspoon ground cinnamon

¼ teaspoon ground cardamom (or the ground seeds from 3 pods)

¼ teaspoon ground cloves

325 g (11 oz) plain (all-purpose) flour, plus extra for dusting

1 teaspoon baking powder

½ teaspoon salt

Line 3 baking sheets with nonstick baking paper. Place the butter and sugar in a large bowl and beat together with a hand-held electric whisk until light and fluffy. Add the egg and spices and beat well. Stir in the flour, baking powder and salt and mix until combined.

Turn the dough out onto a floured surface and knead lightly until smooth. Roll out to 2–3 mm (⅛ inch) thick, then cut out 30–40 shapes, such as stars, or stamp out rounds using a 6 cm (2½ inch) cutter, and place the cookies on the prepared baking sheets

Bake in a preheated oven, 180°C (350°F), Gas Mark 4, for 14–16 minutes until lightly golden and tinged brown around the edges. Transfer to wire racks to cool.

# Peanut Butter Millionaire's Shortbread

VG

*Makes:* 9 squares
*Prep time:* 20 minutes, plus chilling
*Cook time:* 5–6 minutes

50 g (2 oz) rolled oats
50 g (2 oz) ground almonds (almond meal)
2 tablespoons golden syrup or maple syrup
20 g (¾ oz) vegan margarine

**FOR THE TOPPING**

20 g (¾ oz) unsalted peanuts
50 g (2 oz) coconut oil, melted
2 tablespoons golden syrup or maple syrup
175 g (6 oz) smooth peanut butter
100 g (3½ oz) 70% cocoa dark chocolate
sea salt flakes

Line a 20 cm (8 inch) square cake tin (cake pan) with nonstick baking paper in 2 strips, overlapping in a '+' shape.

Put the oats in a dry frying pan (skillet) and place over a medium–high heat. Cook, stirring constantly, until they turn a shade darker and smell toasted. Tip into a bowl. Repeat with the ground almonds, then tip them into the bowl with the oats. Finally, toast the unsalted peanuts for the topping in the same way, then roughly chop them.

Make the shortbread. Melt together the syrup and margarine in a small saucepan. Add the toasted oats and ground almonds and stir well to combine. Press this mixture evenly into the prepared tin and refrigerate while you complete the next stage.

Make the topping. Whisk together the melted coconut oil, syrup and peanut butter. Pour over the prepared base and allow to set in the refrigerator for 1 hour.

Melt the chocolate in a small bowl set over a pan of simmering water, making sure the water does not touch the bottom of the bowl.

Pour the chocolate over the peanut butter layer, smoothing out with the back of a spoon to get it into all the corners. Top with the chopped toasted peanuts and a sprinkle of sea salt flakes, if using.

Refrigerate until the chocolate has set, then cut into 9 squares with a sharp knife. Store in the refrigerator.

# GINGERBREAD PEOPLE

*Makes:* 12–14

***Prep time:* 15 minutes, plus cooling**

***Cook time:* 15–18 minutes**

75 g (3 oz) cold unsalted butter, diced

125 g (4 oz) wholemeal (whole-wheat) plain (all-purpose) flour

125 g (4 oz) self-raising flour, plus extra for dusting

2 teaspoons ground ginger

½ teaspoon ground cinnamon

pinch of ground cloves

75 g (3 oz) soft light brown sugar

1 tablespoon black treacle (molasses)

2 tablespoons golden syrup

1 small egg, lightly beaten

handful of currants, to decorate

Line 2 baking sheets with nonstick baking paper. Place the butter, flours and spices in a food processor and pulse until the mixture resembles fine breadcrumbs. Add the sugar, treacle, golden syrup and egg and pulse until just combined.

Tip the mixture onto a floured surface and knead gently into a smooth dough. Roll out the dough to 3 mm (⅛ inch) thick, then use a cutter to cut into 12–14 large gingerbread person shapes, rerolling the trimmings if necessary to make more shapes.

Place the gingerbread people on the prepared baking sheets and press in currants for eyes. Bake in a preheated oven, 180°C (350°F), Gas Mark 4, for 15–18 minutes until golden. Leave to cool on the sheets for 2–3 minutes, then transfer to wire racks to cool completely.

# GINGER & CHOCOLATE COOKIES

VG

*Makes:* 14

***Prep time:* 20 minutes, plus cooling**

***Cook time:* 10 minutes**

6 tablespoons golden syrup

50 g (2 oz) vegan spread

115 g (4 oz) rolled oats

75 g (3 oz) wholemeal (whole-wheat) plain (all-purpose) flour

1 teaspoon baking powder

50 g (2 oz) well-drained stem ginger in syrup, finely chopped

50 g (2 oz) plain dark chocolate (70% cocoa solids), roughly chopped

Heat the golden syrup and vegan spread in a small saucepan over a gentle heat until melted, stirring. Allow to cool slightly.

Mix all the remaining ingredients together in a large bowl. Pour in the syrup mixture and mix to form a soft dough. Place 14 spoonfuls of the mixture, well spaced apart, on a large baking sheet lined with baking paper and gently press with the back of a spoon to flatten slightly. Bake in a preheated oven, 180°C (350°F), Gas Mark 4, for 8–10 minutes until pale golden.

Leave the cookies to cool on the baking sheet for 5 minutes until firm, then transfer to a wire rack to cool completely.

# MAPLE BISCUITS

*Makes:* 40
*Prep time:* 20 minutes, plus setting
*Cook time:* 12–15 minutes

- 6 tablespoons maple syrup
- 50 g (2 oz) caster (superfine) sugar
- 1 teaspoon bicarbonate of soda (baking soda)
- 1 egg yolk
- 100 g (3½ oz) butter, melted
- 150 g (5 oz) plain (all-purpose) flour
- ¼ teaspoon ground cinnamon
- 75 g (3 oz) plain dark chocolate, broken into pieces
- 75 g (3 oz) white chocolate, broken into pieces

Stir the maple syrup, sugar, bicarbonate of soda and egg yolk into the melted butter, then mix in the flour and cinnamon. Beat to a smooth creamy dough.

Drop teaspoons of the mixture, spaced slightly apart, onto 2 baking sheets lined with nonstick baking paper. Bake in a preheated oven, 190°C (375°F), Gas Mark 5, for 4–5 minutes until golden brown. Leave to harden for 1–2 minutes, then loosen and transfer to a wire rack.

Melt the plain dark and the white chocolate in separate heatproof bowls set over saucepans of simmering water.

Hold a biscuit over one of the bowls and spoon a little of the chocolate over half of it, spreading it with the back of the spoon. Return the biscuit to the wire rack and coat all the biscuits in the same way, so half are covered with dark and the rest with white chocolate. Leave in a cool place for 30 minutes until the chocolate has hardened.

# FLORENTINES

*Makes:* 48
*Prep time:* 30 minutes, plus cooling and setting
*Cook time:* 40 minutes

150 g (5 oz) butter
175 g (6 oz) caster (superfine) sugar
4 tablespoons double (heavy) cream
75 g (3 oz) mixed peel, chopped
50 g (2 oz) glacé cherries, chopped
50 g (2 oz) flaked (slivered) almonds
40 g (1½ oz) dried cranberries
25 g (1 oz) pine nuts
50 g (2 oz) plain (all-purpose) flour
150 g (5 oz) plain dark chocolate
150 g (5 oz) white chocolate

Heat the butter and sugar gently in a pan until the butter is melted. Increase the heat and bring to the boil. Immediately remove the pan from the heat, add the cream, mixed peel, cherries, almonds, cranberries, pine nuts and flour. Stir well until evenly combined.

Line 2 large baking sheets with nonstick baking paper. Drop 12 heaped teaspoonfuls (a quarter of the mixture) onto each of the baking sheets, leaving a 5 cm (2 inch) gap for spreading. Bake in a preheated oven, 180°C (350°F), Gas Mark 4, for 7 minutes.

Remove the baking sheets from the oven. Using a 7 cm (3 inch) cookie cutter, carefully drag the edges of the florentines into neat rounds so that they are about 5 cm (2 inches) across. Bake for a further 3–4 minutes until golden around the edges. Remove from the oven and leave for 2 minutes. Use a palette knife to transfer the florentines to baking paper and leave to cool. Repeat with the remaining mixture.

Melt the plain dark and white chocolate in separate bowls over pans of simmering water. Spoon the melted chocolate into separate piping bags and drizzle over the florentines. Leave to set.

# WHITE CHOCOLATE & NUT BLONDIES

*Makes:* **15 squares**

*Prep time:* **20 minutes**

*Cook time:* **40 minutes**

400 g (13 oz) white chocolate, chopped

75 g (3 oz) slightly salted butter

3 eggs

175 g (6 oz) light muscovado (brown) sugar

150 g (5 oz) self-raising flour

150 g (5 oz) unblanched hazelnuts or Brazil nuts, chopped

Melt 100 g (3½ oz) of the chocolate and the butter in a heatproof bowl set over a saucepan of gently simmering water (don't let the base of the bowl touch the water).

Beat the eggs and sugar in a separate bowl until light and foamy. Stir in the melted chocolate mixture. Tip in the flour, remaining chocolate and the nuts and mix together until just combined.

Spoon the mixture into a lined 28 x 18 cm (11 x 7 inch) shallow baking tin or roasting tin and level the surface. Bake in a preheated oven, 190°C (375°F), Gas Mark 5, for about 35 minutes, or until deep golden and just firm to the touch. Leave to cool in the tin, then transfer to a board and cut into small squares. Peel off the lining paper.

# MILK & COOKIE BROWNIES

(VG)

*Makes:* **8 squares**

*Prep time:* **10 minutes**

*Cook time:* **15 minutes, plus cooling**

300 g (10 oz) chocolate sandwich cookies, such as Oreos, plus 5 extra, roughly chopped (optional)

300 ml (½ pint) dairy-free milk

1½ teaspoons baking powder

Line the base of a 22 x 18 cm (8½ x 7 inch) cake tin (cake pan) with baking paper.

Blitz the cookies in a food processor to a fine crumb, then add the milk and baking powder and blitz until smooth.

Pour the batter into the prepared tin and top with the extra chopped cookies, if using. Bake in a preheated oven, 180°C (350°F), Gas Mark 4, for 15 minutes, or until a skewer inserted in the centre comes out clean. Allow to cool before slicing into 8 squares.

# CLASSIC CHOCOLATE BROWNIES

*Makes:* 8–10 squares
*Prep time:* 10 minutes
*Cook time:* 30 minutes

125 g (4 oz) butter, plus extra for greasing
2 eggs
125 g (4 oz) soft light brown sugar
75 g (3 oz) self-raising flour
50 g (2 oz) cocoa powder, sieved, plus extra to decorate
50 g (2 oz) plain dark chocolate, chopped
1 teaspoon chocolate extract
salt

Grease and line an 18 cm (7 inch) square deep cake tin (cake pan).

Beat together the sunflower spread, eggs and sugar. Stir in the flour and cocoa powder, then add the chocolate and chocolate extract. Stir in 1 teaspoon boiling water and a pinch of salt.

Transfer the mixture to the prepared tin. Bake in a preheated oven, 190°C (375°F), Gas Mark 5, for 30 minutes, or until a skewer inserted into the centre comes out clean.

Leave to cool in the tin, then cut into squares. Dust with a little cocoa powder to serve.

# FRYING PAN CHOCOLATE BROWNIES

*Makes:* 8 squares
*Prep time:* 10 minutes
*Cook time:* 30 minutes

200 g (7 oz) butter
200 g (7 oz) dark chocolate, chopped
175 g (6 oz) soft dark brown sugar
150 g (5 oz) caster (superfine) sugar
4 eggs
50 g (2 oz) ground almonds (almond meal)
75 g (3 oz) plain (all-purpose) flour
vanilla ice cream, to serve

Gently melt the butter and chocolate together in a 23 cm (9 inch) ovenproof frying pan (skillet). Remove from the heat and cool for a couple of minutes.

Beat together the sugars and eggs, then stir in the chocolate mixture followed by the almonds and flour.

Wipe the rim of the frying pan with a damp piece of kitchen paper (paper towel) or cloth to neaten, then pour the mixture into the pan. Bake in a preheated oven, 180°C (350°F), Gas Mark 4, for 25 minutes until just set. Serve warm with vanilla ice cream.

# Salted Caramel Crunch Brownies

*Makes:* 12–16 squares
*Prep time:* 10 minutes, plus cooling
*Cook time:* 20 minutes

- 150 g (5 oz) unsalted butter
- 150 g (5 oz) plain dark chocolate, broken into small pieces
- 100 g (3½ oz) dulce de leche or thick caramel sauce
- 2 large eggs
- 75 g (3 oz) soft dark brown sugar
- 75 g (3 oz) caster (superfine) sugar
- ¼ teaspoon salt
- 50 g (2 oz) self-raising flour
- 100 g (3½ oz) walnut pieces, chopped
- 1 teaspoon sea salt flakes

Line a 30 x 20 cm (12 x 8 inch) brownie tin with nonstick baking paper. Place the butter and chocolate in a small saucepan over a low heat and warm until just melted. In a separate saucepan, gently warm through the dulce de leche or caramel sauce.

Meanwhile, place the eggs, brown sugar, caster sugar and salt in a large bowl and whisk until combined. Using a rubber spatula, stir in the melted chocolate, flour and half the walnuts.

Scrape the mixture into the prepared tin. Scatter over the remaining walnuts, then drizzle with the dulce de leche or caramel sauce and sprinkle with the sea salt flakes.

Bake in a preheated oven, 200°C (400°F), Gas Mark 6, for 15–18 minutes until just firm to the touch, but with a slightly fudgy texture.

Leave to cool in the tin for 1–2 minutes, then lift onto a board using the baking paper and cut into 12–16 squares. Serve warm or cold.

# MINI CHOCOLATE LOGS

***Makes:*** **6**
***Prep time:*** **20 minutes**
***Cook time:*** **10 minutes**

- 3 eggs
- 125 g (4 oz) golden caster (superfine) sugar, plus 2 tablespoons for sprinkling
- 100 g (3½ oz) plain (all-purpose) flour
- 25 g (1 oz) cocoa powder
- 1 tablespoon hot water
- 6 tablespoons shop-bought chocolate spread

Whisk the eggs with the sugar for 10 minutes until thick. Sift over the flour and cocoa powder and gently fold in, along with the hot water.

Line a 33 x 23 cm (13 x 9 inch) Swiss roll tin with nonstick baking paper. Pour the mixture into the tin. Bake in a preheated oven, 220°C (425°F), Gas Mark 7, for 10 minutes until risen and just firm.

Sprinkle a large sheet of nonstick baking paper with sugar. Upturn the cake onto the baking paper and carefully peel off the lining. Use a sharp knife to trim off all the crisp edges.

Cut the cake in half to make 2 long strips, then cut each strip into 3 pieces. As you cut the cake, cut the nonstick baking paper underneath as well, using a ruler to make sure all the strips are an equal width. Spread each piece of cake with 1 tablespoon of chocolate spread. Roll up each cake and remove the baking paper before serving.

# Mulled Wine Biscuits

*Makes:* about 25
*Prep time:* 15 minutes, plus cooling
*Cook time:* 25–30 minutes

140 g (4½ oz) raisins
75 g (3 oz) dried cranberries
150 ml (¼ pint) red wine
100 g (3½ oz) redcurrant jelly
pinch of chilli powder
1 teaspoon ground cinnamon
¼ teaspoon ground cloves
50 g (2 oz) walnuts, chopped
50 g (2 oz) blanched almonds, chopped
100 g (3½ oz) plain dark chocolate, finely chopped
75 g (3 oz) self-raising flour
finely grated rind of 1 orange
50 g (2 oz) unsalted butter, melted, plus extra for greasing
1 egg
icing (confectioners') sugar, for dusting

Put the raisins and cranberries in a small heavy-based saucepan with the wine, redcurrant jelly and spices. Heat until the jelly dissolves, then bring to the boil and boil for 2–3 minutes until the syrup is reduced by about half. Allow to cool.

Mix the nuts and chocolate in a bowl with the flour, orange rind, butter, egg and fruit mixture to make a paste. Place teaspoons of the mixture, spaced slightly apart, on a lightly greased baking sheet.

Bake in a preheated oven, 180°C (350°F), Gas Mark 4, for about 20 minutes until they have spread slightly. Leave them on the baking sheet for 3 minutes, then transfer to a wire rack to cool. Dust generously with icing sugar.

# Pistachio Nut Stollen

*Serves:* 15
*Prep time:* 40 minutes, plus rising
*Cook time:* 50–60 minutes

- 625 g (1¼ lb) strong plain (all-purpose) flour
- 25 g (1 oz) fresh yeast, crumbled
- 300 ml (½ pint) lukewarm milk
- 75 g (3 oz) caster (superfine) sugar
- 1 egg
- 1 teaspoon vanilla extract
- grated rind of ½ lemon
- ½ teaspoon salt
- 175 g (6 oz) butter
- 175 g (6 oz) cut mixed peel
- 125 g (4 oz) pistachio nuts
- 175 g (6 oz) icing (confectioners') sugar
- 1 tablespoon maraschino liqueur
- 125 g (4 oz) marzipan
- 65 g (2½ oz) melted butter, to glaze

Sift 500 g (1 lb) of the flour into a bowl, reserving a little sifted flour for sprinkling. Make a well, add the yeast and milk and stir into the flour. Sprinkle with a little flour, cover the bowl and leave for 20 minutes.

Add the sugar, egg, vanilla extract, lemon rind and salt to the yeast and knead to give a dry, firm dough. Cover the bowl and leave to rise for 10 minutes.

Work the butter together with the remaining flour and the mixed peel. Work this mixture into the dough and leave to rise for a further 30 minutes.

Work the pistachios, 50 g (2 oz) of the icing sugar and the maraschino into the marzipan. Roll out to 1 cm (½ inch) thick and cut into 1 cm (½ inch) cubes. Work these quickly into the dough. Shape the dough into 2 balls, then roll into 2 stollen about 30 cm (12 inches) long. Place on a baking sheet lined with greaseproof paper (wax paper). Cover with greased clingfilm (plastic wrap) and leave to rise for 20–30 minutes.

Bake in a preheated oven, 200°C (400°F), Gas Mark 6, for 50–60 minutes, or until a skewer inserted into the centre comes out clean. Brush the warm stollen all over with melted butter and dust with the remaining icing sugar.

# TOFFEE APPLE MINI TRAYBAKES

*Makes:* 12
*Prep time:* 10 minutes
*Cook time:* 20 minutes

- 125 g (4 oz) unsalted butter, softened, plus extra for greasing
- 125 g (4 oz) self-raising flour
- 1 teaspoon baking powder
- 1 teaspoon ground cinnamon
- ¼ teaspoon ground nutmeg
- ½ teaspoon ground ginger
- 75 g (3 oz) soft dark brown sugar
- 50 g (2 oz) caster (superfine) sugar
- 2 large eggs, lightly beaten
- crème fraîche, to serve (optional)

### FOR THE TOFFEE APPLES

- 50 g (2 oz) demerara sugar
- 50 g (2 oz) unsalted butter
- 2 teaspoons lemon juice
- 3 dessert apples, peeled, cored and sliced

Grease a traybake tray or 12-hole nonstick muffin tin. Sift the flour, baking powder and spices into a large bowl. Add the remaining ingredients and beat together with a handheld electric whisk until smooth and creamy. Spoon the mixture into the prepared tin

Bake in a preheated oven, 200°C (400°F), Gas Mark 6, for 12–15 minutes until risen and firm to the touch.

Meanwhile, make the toffee apples. Place the sugar, butter and lemon juice in a nonstick frying pan (skillet) over a medium heat and heat until melted. Add the apples and simmer for 7–8 minutes, turning occasionally, until golden and softened. Leave to cool slightly.

Remove the cakes from the oven and transfer to a wire rack to cool slightly. Serve warm, topped with the toffee apples and sauce, and with crème fraîche, if liked.

# STICKY TOFFEE & DATE SQUARES

*Makes:* 24 squares
*Prep time:* 25 minutes, plus cooling
*Cook time:* 55 minutes

- 225 g (7½ oz) stoned (pitted) dates, chopped
- 150 ml (¼ pint) water
- 150 ml (¼ pint) double (heavy) cream
- 175 g (6 oz) light muscovado (brown) sugar
- 200 g (7 oz) lightly salted butter, softened
- 100 g (3½ oz) caster (superfine) sugar
- 2 teaspoons vanilla bean paste
- 3 eggs
- 175 g (6 oz) self-raising flour
- ½ teaspoon baking powder

Line a 28 x 18 cm (11 x 7 inch) shallow baking tin with nonstick baking paper. Put 125 g (4 oz) of the dates in a saucepan with the measurement water and bring to the boil. Reduce the heat and cook gently for 5 minutes, or until the dates are pulpy. Transfer to a bowl and leave to cool. Put the cream, muscovado sugar and 75 g (3 oz) of the butter in a small saucepan and heat gently until the sugar dissolves. Bring to the boil and boil for 5 minutes, or until thickened and caramelized. Leave to cool.

Put the remaining butter in a bowl with the caster sugar, vanilla bean paste and eggs, sift in the flour and baking powder and beat with a hand-held electric whisk until pale and creamy. Beat in the cooked dates and 100 ml (3½ fl oz) of the caramel mixture. Spoon into the prepared tin and level the surface. Scatter with the remaining dates.

Bake in a preheated oven, 180°C (350°F), Gas Mark 4, for 25 minutes, or until just firm. Spoon the remaining caramel on top and return to the oven for 15 minutes until the caramel has firmed. Transfer to a wire rack to cool.

# SPICY APPLE PARKIN

*Makes:* 12 slices
*Prep time:* 20 minutes, plus cooling
*Cook time:* 1–1 hour 10 minutes

- 4 tart dessert apples, such as Granny Smith
- 5 tablespoons apple juice
- ¼ teaspoon ground cloves
- 100 g (3½ oz) self-raising wholemeal (whole-wheat) flour
- 100 g (3½ oz) self-raising white flour
- 175 g (6 oz) medium oatmeal
- 1 teaspoon bicarbonate of soda (baking soda)
- 2 teaspoons ground ginger
- 175 g (6 oz) black treacle (molasses)
- 150 g (5 oz) golden syrup
- 75 g (3 oz) unsalted butter, softened, plus extra for greasing

Peel, core and slice the apples and put the slices in a small saucepan with the apple juice and ground cloves. Bring to the boil, reduce the heat and cook gently, uncovered, for about 5 minutes, or until the apples have softened slightly. Drain and leave to cool.

Put the flours, oatmeal, bicarbonate of soda and ginger in a mixing bowl. Add the treacle, golden syrup and butter and mix together. Stir in the apples, then pour into a greased deep 20 x 30 cm (8 x 12 inches) baking tin, its base and 2 long sides also lined with greaseproof paper (wax paper).

Bake in a preheated oven, 160°C (325°F), Gas Mark 3, for 55 minutes–1 hour, until well risen and a skewer inserted into the centre comes out clean. Leave to cool for 10 minutes, then loosen the edges, turn out onto a wire rack, peel off the lining paper and leave to cool completely.

# STICKY GINGERBREAD

*Makes:* 12 bars
*Prep time:* 20 minutes
*Cook time:* 40 minutes

- 225 g (7½ oz) plain (all-purpose) flour
- 1 teaspoon bicarbonate of soda (baking soda)
- 2 teaspoons ground ginger
- 75 g (3 oz) lightly salted butter
- 125 g (4 oz) light muscovado (brown) sugar
- 75 g (3 oz) golden syrup
- 75 g (3 oz) black treacle
- 125 ml (4 fl oz) buttermilk
- 1 egg, beaten
- 75 g (3 oz) sultanas

### FOR THE GLAZE

- 3 tablespoons ginger marmalade or jam (jelly)

Put the flour, bicarbonate of soda and ginger into a bowl. Put the butter, sugar, golden syrup and treacle into a saucepan and heat gently without boiling until the butter has melted. Remove from the heat and stir in the buttermilk, then beat in the egg. Add to the dry ingredients with the sultanas and beat well to mix.

Spoon the mixture into a lined 20 cm (8 inch) square cake tin (cake pan) or shallow baking tin, spreading the mixture into the corners. Bake in a preheated oven, 160°C (325°F), Gas Mark 3, for about 30 minutes, or until risen, just firm to the touch and a skewer inserted into the centre comes out clean. Leave to cool in the tin (the cake might sink slightly in the centre), then transfer to a board and peel off the lining paper.

Make the glaze. Put the marmalade or jam and 1 tablespoon of water in a small saucepan and heat gently. Press through a sieve (strainer) to remove any lumps and brush over the gingerbread, then cut into bars.

# Panforte di Siena

*Serves:* 15
*Prep time:* 20 minutes, plus cooling
*Cook time:* 55 minutes

75 g (3 oz) hazelnuts, toasted, skinned and chopped

75 g (3 oz) blanched almonds, toasted and chopped

75 g (3 oz) candied orange peel, chopped

75 g (3 oz) candied lemon peel, chopped

75 g (3 oz) candied fruit, chopped

2 teaspoons ground cinnamon

large pinch of ground mixed spice

75 g (3 oz) plain (all-purpose) flour

125 g (4 oz) thick honey

100 g (3½ oz) caster (superfine) sugar

icing (confectioners') sugar, for dusting

Line a deep sponge cake tin (cake pan) or a loose-bottomed 18–20 cm (7–8 inch) round cake tin with rice paper. Combine the nuts, peel and fruit, then sift in the spices and flour and stir until evenly mixed.

Put the honey and sugar into a saucepan and bring slowly to the boil. Pour over the nut mixture and stir well until blended and a sticky mass forms.

Spoon the mixture into the prepared tin, but don't press down too firmly. Bake in a preheated oven, 150°C (300°F), Gas Mark 2, for about 50 minutes, or until almost firm to the touch.

Cool in the tin and then remove carefully. If the rice paper is torn or pulled away from the cake, add a new layer, attaching it with a dab of lightly beaten egg white. Dust the top heavily with icing sugar and serve cut into thin wedges.

# DATE & SESAME BARS

*Makes:* 16 bars

*Prep time:* 15 minutes

*Cook time:* 25–30 minutes

125 g (4 oz) unsalted butter, diced, plus extra for greasing

75 g (3 oz) golden caster (superfine) sugar

1 tablespoon clear honey

150 g (5 oz) stoned (pitted) dates, chopped

125 g (4 oz) self-raising flour

125 g (4 oz) medium oatmeal

50 g (2 oz) sesame seeds

Put the butter, sugar and honey in a saucepan and heat gently until the butter has melted, then remove from the heat and stir in the dates.

Place the flour and oatmeal in a bowl. Add the sesame seeds, reserving 2 tablespoons, then pour in the butter mixture and mix until combined.

Spoon into a greased 28 x 18 cm (11 x 7 inch) shallow baking tin and level the surface. Scatter with the reserved seeds. Bake in a preheated oven, 180°C (350°F), Gas Mark 4, for 20–25 minutes or until pale golden and firm to the touch. Leave to cool in the tin, then turn out on to a board and cut into bars.

# LAYERED NUTTY BARS

*Makes:* 10 bars

*Prep time:* 20 minutes, plus chilling

*Cook time:* 5 minutes

50 g (2 oz) butter

400 g (13 oz) fat-free sweetened condensed milk

200 g (7 oz) plain dark chocolate, broken into pieces

125 g (4 oz) rich tea biscuits (cookies)

50 g (2 oz) hazelnuts

100 g (3½ oz) shelled pistachio nuts

Use some of the butter to grease the base and sides of a 20 cm (8 inch) round spring-form tin. Put the rest of the butter in a saucepan with the condensed milk and chocolate. Heat gently for 3–4 minutes, stirring until melted, then remove from the heat.

Place the biscuits in a plastic bag and crush roughly into chunky pieces using a rolling pin. Toast the hazelnuts under a preheated hot grill (brolier) until lightly browned, then roughly chop with the pistachios.

Stir the biscuits into the chocolate mixture then spoon half the mixture into the prepared tin and spread level. Reserve 2 tablespoons of the nuts for the top, then sprinkle the rest over the chocolate biscuit layer. Cover with the remaining chocolate biscuit mixture, level the surface with the back of the spoon and sprinkle with the reserved nuts.

Chill the nut mixture for 3–4 hours until firm, then loosen the edges and remove the sides of the tin. Cut into 10 thin slices.

# CARAMEL PINE NUT SLICE

*Makes:* 15 slices
*Prep time:* 20 minutes, plus chilling
*Cook time:* 15 minutes

100 g (3½ oz) butter, at room temperature

50 g (2 oz) caster (superfine) sugar

100 g (3½ oz) brown rice flour

100 g (3½ oz) cornflour (cornstarch)

grated rind of ½ orange

### FOR THE CARAMEL

100 g (3½ oz) butter

50 g (2 oz) soft light brown sugar

397 g (13 oz) can condensed milk

50 g (2 oz) pine nuts

### FOR THE TOPPING

100 g (3½ oz) plain dark chocolate, broken into pieces

Beat the butter and sugar together in a bowl until pale and creamy, then stir in the flours and orange rind until well combined. Press the shortbread into a 28 x 18 cm (11 x 7 inch) baking tin. Bake in a preheated oven, 200°C (400°F), Gas Mark 6, for 10–12 minutes until golden.

Meanwhile, make the caramel. Put the butter, sugar and condensed milk in a heavy-based saucepan and heat over a low heat until the sugar has dissolved, then cook for 5 minutes, stirring continuously until just beginning to darken. Stir in the pine nuts, then remove from the heat and leave to cool a little. Pour the caramel over the shortbread base and leave to cool completely.

Make the topping. Melt the chocolate in a heatproof bowl set over a saucepan of simmering water. When the caramel is firm, drizzle the melted chocolate randomly over the top so that the caramel can still be seen. Refrigerate until set, then cut into 15 pieces.

# ICED FIG SLICE

*Makes:* 12 slices
*Prep time:* 25 minutes
*Cook time:* 1 hour

225 g (7½ oz) ready-made puff pastry

175 g (6 oz) slightly salted butter, softened, plus extra for greasing

175 g (6 oz) caster (superfine) sugar

200 g (7 oz) self-raising flour, plus extra for dusting

½ teaspoon baking powder

3 eggs

6 figs, quartered

### FOR THE ICING

100 g (3½ oz) icing (confectioners') sugar, sifted

1 tablespoon lemon juice

Roll out the pastry on a lightly floured surface and use to line a greased 23 cm (9 inch) square shallow baking tin or small roasting tin. Line the pastry case with greaseproof paper (wax paper) and fill with baking beans. Bake in a preheated oven, 200°C (400°F), Gas Mark 6, for 15 minutes.

Remove from the oven and remove the paper and beans. Reduce the oven temperature to 180°C (350°F), Gas Mark 4.

Beat together the butter, sugar, flour, baking powder and eggs in a bowl until pale and creamy. Spoon over the pastry base and level the surface. Arrange the figs over the top. Bake in the oven for about 45 minutes, or until risen and golden. Leave to cool in the tin.

Make the icing. Beat together the icing sugar and lemon juice in a bowl to make a smooth, spoonable icing. If necessary, beat in a dash of water or extra lemon juice. Drizzle the icing over the cake, then cut into squares or fingers.

# HONEY & GINGER FLAPJACKS

***Makes:*** **12**

***Prep time:*** **10 minutes, plus cooling**

***Cook time:*** **30 minutes**

50 g (2 oz) soft light brown sugar

150 g (5 oz) butter

50 g (2 oz) clear honey

200 g (7 oz) millet flakes or porridge oats (oatmeal)

2 tablespoons mixed seeds, such as pumpkin and sunflower

1 piece of stem ginger, finely chopped

Place the sugar, butter and honey in a heavy-based saucepan and heat until melted, then add the millet flakes or porridge oats and seeds. Stir in the stem ginger.

Spoon the mixture into a 28 x 18 cm (11 x 7 inch) nonstick baking tin and press down lightly. Bake in a preheated oven, 150°C (300°F), Gas Mark 2, for 30 minutes.

Using a knife, gently score into 12 pieces and leave to cool in the tin. Remove from the tin, then cut or break into individual pieces along the score lines.

# MARSHMALLOW CRACKLE SQUARES

***Makes:*** **14**

***Prep time:*** **10 minutes, plus setting**

***Cook time:*** **5 minutes**

200 g (7 oz) pink and white marshmallows, halved

40 g (1½ oz) unsalted butter, diced

100 g (3½ oz) crisped rice cereal

pink sugar sprinkles, to decorate

Reserve 50 g (2 oz) of the white marshmallows. Put 25 g (1 oz) of the butter and the remaining marshmallows into a saucepan and heat very gently until melted. Remove from the heat and stir in the cereal until evenly coated.

Spoon the mixture into an 18 cm (7 inch) square shallow baking tin, lined with baking parchment, and pack down firmly with the back of a lightly oiled spoon.

Place the remaining butter and reserved marshmallows in a small saucepan and heat gently until melted. Drizzle into the tin in lines, then scatter the sprinkles over the top. Leave in a cool place for 2 hours, or until firm.

Turn out of the tin onto a board, peel off the lining paper and cut into squares.

# LITTLE TREATS

# Rocky Road Clusters

*Makes:* 24
*Prep time:* 40 minutes, plus setting
*Cook time:* 10 minutes

- 150 g (5 oz) mixed whole nuts (such as cashews, hazelnuts, pistachios)
- 300 g (10 oz) plain dark chocolate, broken into pieces
- 15 g (½ oz) unsalted butter
- 2 tablespoons icing (confectioners') sugar
- 2 tablespoons double (heavy) cream

Put the nuts on a piece of foil on a baking sheet, then toast under a preheated hot grill (broiler) for 3–4 minutes until golden. Allow to cool slightly, then chop roughly.

Melt 75 g (3 oz) of the chocolate in a heatproof bowl over a pan of gently simmering water. Stir the butter, sugar and cream into the melted chocolate until smooth and glossy, then mix in all but 2 tablespoons of the chopped nuts.

Drop teaspoons of the mixture on to a baking sheet lined with nonstick baking paper. Chill for 2–3 hours until the mixture is firm.

Line 2 x 12-hole muffin tins with petit four cases. Melt the remaining chocolate as before. Coat the nut clusters in the melted chocolate by holding them on a fork, one at a time, over the bowl of chocolate and spooning some of it over the top with a teaspoon.

When the excess chocolate has dripped away, place the cluster in one of the petit-four cases. Repeat with the remainder.

Put the chocolates in a cool place and leave to set for at least 1 hour, then sprinkle with the reserved nuts. They will keep in the refrigerator for up to 4 days.

# MINT & CHOCOLATE FUDGE

*Makes:* 36 pieces
*Prep time:* 15 minutes, plus setting
*Cook time:* 5 minutes

40 g (1½ oz) strong peppermints
500 g (1 lb) plain dark chocolate, chopped
400 g (13 oz) can sweetened condensed milk
50 g (2 oz) milk chocolate or white chocolate, melted

Place the peppermints in a plastic food bag and crush them with a rolling pin, breaking them into small pieces. Continue to roll and flatten the mints until they are ground to a powder. Line a shallow 18 cm (7 inch) baking tin with nonstick baking paper.

Put the plain dark chocolate and condensed milk in a heatproof bowl over a pan of gently simmering water. Stir until melted, then stir in the peppermints.

Beat the mixture until the ingredients are combined then turn it into the tin, spreading it into the corners. Level the surface and leave to cool. Chill in the refrigerator for at least 2 hours.

Lift the fudge out of the tin and peel off the paper. Melt the milk or white chocolate in a heatproof bowl over a pan of gently simmering water, then place in a piping bag. Snip off the tip and scribble lines of chocolate over the fudge. When the chocolate is set, cut the fudge into 2 cm (¾ inch) squares. It will keep for up to 2 weeks in the refrigerator.

# JAFFA ORANGE FUDGE

*Makes:* 36 pieces
*Prep time:* 10 minutes, plus setting
*Cook time:* 15 minutes

125 g (4 oz) butter
200 ml (7 fl oz) evaporated milk
450 g (14½ oz) caster (superfine) sugar
2 teaspoons vanilla extract
50 ml (2 fl oz) water
75 g (3 oz) orange-flavoured dark chocolate, chopped
pinch of ground cinnamon
small pinch of grated nutmeg
vegetable oil, for greasing
8 chocolate orange cakes, chopped

Heat the butter, evaporated milk, sugar, vanilla extract and measurement water gently together in a heavy-based saucepan, stirring until the sugar has dissolved. Bring to the boil.

Boil the mixture for 10 minutes, stirring all the time (test to see if it is ready by carefully dropping ½ teaspoon of the mixture into cold water – it should form a soft ball). Quickly pour half the fudge mixture into a heatproof jug (pitcher). Add the chocolate, cinnamon and nutmeg to the pan and stir to melt.

Grease a 500 g (1 lb) loaf tin (loaf pan). Pour half the chocolate fudge into the base of the tin, then scatter over the cakes. Pour the vanilla fudge on top, then finish with a final layer of chocolate fudge. Cool, cover with clingfilm (plastic wrap) and chill overnight.

Turn out the fudge and cut into pieces.

# BOOZY GINGER CHOCS

(VG)

*Makes:* 12

*Prep time:* 20 minutes, plus freezing

*Cook time:* 5 minutes

3 pieces of stem ginger, drained

1 tablespoon spiced whisky liqueur

200 g (7 oz) orange-flavoured dark chocolate

Polish a flexible ice-cube tray with 12 or more sections using kitchen paper (paper towel), then place in the freezer.

Cut each piece of stem ginger into quarters and place in a small bowl with the whisky liqueur.

Melt the chocolate in a bowl over a pan of simmering water, making sure that the water doesn't touch the bottom of the bowl. Half-fill each section of the ice-cube tray with the melted chocolate. Add a piece of macerated stem ginger, then pour the rest of the melted chocolate on top. Return to the freezer for 30 minutes.

Turn out the chocolates onto a piece of waxed paper to serve. Alternatively, chill in the refrigerator until ready to serve.

# CREAMY PISTACHIO TOFFEE

*Makes:* 30

*Prep time:* 15 minutes, plus setting

*Cook time:* 20 minutes

300 g (10 oz) granulated sugar

300 ml (½ pint) double (heavy) cream

25 g (1 oz) unsalted butter, pluis extra for greasing

50 g (2 oz) pistachio nuts, roughly chopped

Put the sugar and cream in a saucepan and heat gently, stirring occasionally, until the sugar has completely dissolved. Stir in the butter, insert a sugar thermometer if you have one, and increase the heat. Cook for about 15 minutes until the temperature reaches 120°C (250°F), or a little of the toffee forms a hard ball when dropped into a bowl of cold water. Stir occasionally at first, then more frequently as the mixture begins to colour, froth and thicken. When the butter begins to separate out of the toffee, it is almost ready. Cook for a few more minutes until it changes to a smooth, glossy toffee.

Remove from the heat, quickly stir in the pistachio nuts, then pour the toffee into a greased 18 cm (7 inch) shallow square cake tin (cake pan). Allow to cool for 5 minutes, then score into strips and leave to cool.

Loosen the edges of the toffee from the sides of the tin and turn it out. Break into pieces with a toffee hammer. The toffee will keep, in an airtight container in a cool place, for up to 1 week.

# GLAZED CHOCOLATE GINGER HEARTS

*Makes:* 24
*Prep time:* 30 minutes, plus chilling and setting
*Cook time:* 15 minutes

125 g (4 oz) butter, plus extra for greasing

125 g (4 oz) caster (superfine) sugar

1 egg

125 g (4 oz) black treacle (molasses)

400 g (13 oz) self-raising flour

2 teaspoons ground ginger

### TO DECORATE

200 g (7 oz) plain dark chocolate

200 g (7 oz) milk chocolate

12 white chocolate buttons

Beat together the butter and sugar until pale and creamy. Add the egg and treacle. Sift the flour and ginger into the bowl and mix to form a firm dough. Knead lightly and chill for 30 minutes.

Lightly grease 2 baking sheets. Roll out the dough to a thickness of 1 cm (⅓ inch) and cut out heart shapes using a biscuit (cookie) cutter. Reroll the trimmings to make more hearts. Bake in a preheated oven, 180°C (350°F), Gas Mark 4, for about 10 minutes until slightly risen. Transfer to a wire rack and leave to cool.

Melt the plain dark and milk chocolate in separate bowls over pans of simmering water. Using a dessertspoon, spoon the plain dark chocolate over about half the hearts, reserving a little for decoration. Lay a white chocolate button in the centre of half the coated hearts. Now use the milk chocolate to cover the remaining hearts, again reserving a little and laying a white chocolate button in the centre of half the coated hearts.

Put the reserved milk chocolate in a piping bag fitted with a fine nozzle and pipe wavy lines over the hearts covered with plain dark chocolate. Use the reserved plain dark chocolate to decorate the hearts covered with milk chocolate. Leave to set.

# PINE NUT PRALINE

*Makes:* about 20 pieces
*Prep time:* 15 minutes, plus setting
*Cook time:* 10 minutes

50 g (2 oz) pine nuts
25 g (1 oz) flaked (slivered) almonds
200 g (7 oz) caster (superfine) sugar
5 tablespoons water
50 g (2 oz) plain dark chocolate, broken into pieces
butter, for greasing

Lightly toast the pine nuts and almonds. Break up the nuts in a food processor or use a pestle and mortar until the nuts are broken into slightly smaller pieces, but not too finely ground.

Put the sugar and measurement water in a small heavy-based saucepan and heat very gently, stirring until the sugar dissolves. Bring to the boil and cook, without stirring, until the syrup has turned to golden caramel. This will take 6–8 minutes. Immediately dip the base of the pan in cold water to prevent further cooking (if you overcook it, the resulting praline will taste bitter) and stir in the nuts.

Work quickly as you turn the praline on to a lightly greased baking sheet, spreading it out in a thin layer before it starts to set. Leave for about 1 hour, until the praline is brittle.

Melt the chocolate in a heatproof bowl over a pan of gently simmering water. Break the praline into pieces and place on a wire rack. Drizzle with the melted chocolate, then leave to set. The praline will keep, in an airtight container in a cool place, for up to 1 week.

# HAZELNUT MERINGUES

*Makes:* about 25
*Prep time:* 20 minutes
*Cook time:* 45–60 minutes

100 g (3½ oz) hazelnuts
4 egg whites
225 g (7½ oz) caster (superfine) sugar
½ teaspoon white wine vinegar
¼ teaspoon vanilla extract
100 g (3½ oz) crème fraîche
175 g (6 oz) redcurrants

Line a baking sheet with nonstick baking paper. Coarsely grind the hazelnuts in a food processor (or chop them and then crush with a pestle and mortar), then set them aside.

Whisk the egg whites in a large bowl until they form soft peaks. Gradually add the sugar, a teaspoon at a time, whisking until the mixture is very stiff and shiny. The mixture should stay put, even when the bowl is tilted. Fold in the vinegar and vanilla extract, then fold in the ground nuts.

Spoon the meringue mixture onto the prepared baking sheet, to make approximately 25 mini meringues, spacing them apart as they will expand slightly in the oven. Bake in a preheated oven, 110°C (225°F), Gas Mark ¼, for 45–60 minutes, or until the meringues are firm and may be easily peeled off the paper.

Allow to cool on the baking sheet. Serve the cooled meringues topped with a little crème fraîche and a small sprig of redcurrants.

# DATE & PISTACHIO TRUFFLES

*Makes:* 16
*Prep time:* 15 minutes
*Cook time:* 1–2 minutes

225 g (7½ oz) shelled pistachio nuts
225 g (7½ oz) stoned (pitted) dates, chopped
1 tablespoon orange blossom water
1 teaspoon ground cinnamon
1 tablespoon clear honey
50 g (2 oz) desiccated coconut (dried shredded coconut)

Dry-fry the pistachios in a heavy-based frying pan (skillet) over a medium heat for 1–2 minutes until they begin to colour and emit a nutty aroma. Put into a food processor with the dates and blend to a thick paste.

Transfer the paste to a bowl and knead in the orange blossom water, cinnamon and honey. Roll 16 small pieces of the mixture into bite-sized balls.

Sprinkle the coconut onto a plate. Roll the truffles in the coconut until evenly coated. Serve with coffee or tea.

# SALTED CARAMEL SHARDS

*Makes:* about 10 pieces
*Cook time:* 10 minutes, plus cooling

100 g (3½ oz) caster (superfine) sugar
1 teaspoon coarse sea salt
chocolate ice cream, to serve

Line a baking sheet with nonstick baking paper. Place the sugar in a small heavy-based saucepan over a low heat. Do not stir. Watch the sugar until the bottom layer has melted, then reduce the heat and stir until the sugar has dissolved and is a light caramel colour.

Pour onto the baking sheet, sprinkle with the sea salt and leave to harden.

When set, after about 10 minutes, use a rolling pin to break into shards.

Serve with chocolate ice cream or as a decoration for fools or syllabubs.

# CHOCOLATE TOFFEE POPCORN

*Serves:* 4
*Prep time:* 15 minutes
*Cook time:* 8–10 minutes

50 g (2 oz) milk chocolate, broken into pieces
50 g (2 oz) firm toffees
4 tablespoons milk
1 tablespoon vegetable oil
75 g (3 oz) popcorn kernels

Melt the chocolate in a small heatproof bowl over a small saucepan of simmering water.

Unwrap the toffees and put them in a plastic food bag. Place on a chopping board and tap firmly with a rolling pin until the toffees have broken into small pieces. Tip the pieces into a small saucepan and add the milk. Cook on the lowest possible heat until the toffee has melted (this will take several minutes, depending on the firmness of the toffee). Remove from the heat.

Put the oil in a large saucepan with a tight-fitting lid and heat for 1 minute. Add the popcorn kernels and cover with the lid. Cook until the popping sound stops, then tip the corn out onto a large baking sheet or roasting tin and leave for 5 minutes.

Using a teaspoon, drizzle lines of the toffee sauce over the corn until lightly coated. Drizzle with lines of chocolate in the same way.

# CARAMELIZED NUTS

*Makes:* about 250g (9 oz)
*Prep time:* 10 minutes
*Cook time:* 15 minutes

150 g (5 oz) unblanched almonds or pistachios
100 g (3½ oz) caster (superfine) sugar
1 tablespoon groundnut oil

Heat a nonstick frying pan (skillet) over very low heat.

Add the almonds or pistachios and sugar and allow the sugar to melt, stirring from time to time with a wooden spatula until the sugar turns to caramel.

Oil a baking tray (baking sheet) with the groundnut oil, then take spoonfuls of nuts and form into small clusters on the tray.

Once the nuts are cold, transfer them from the tray to a serving plate.

# PUDDINGS & DESSERTS

# Roasted Pears with Sugar & Spice

*Serves:* 4
*Prep time:* 20 minutes
*Cook time:* 25 minutes

4 pears
8 tablespoons dry or sweet sherry
6–8 pieces star anise
1 cinnamon stick, broken into pieces
8 cloves
8 cardamom pods, crushed
50 g (2 oz) unsalted butter
4 tablespoons light muscovado (brown) sugar
1 orange
crème fraîche or Greek yogurt, to serve

Leave the peel on the pears and cut them in half, down through the stems to the base. Scoop out the core, then put in a roasting tin with the cut sides up. Spoon the sherry into the cavity of each pear and 8 tablespoons of water into the base of the tin. Sprinkle the spices over the pears, including the cardamom pods and their black seeds. Dot with the butter, then sprinkle with the sugar.

Remove the rind from the orange and sprinkle into the tin. Cut the orange into wedges and squeeze the juice over the pears. Add the wedges to the roasting tin.

Cook in a preheated oven, 180°C (350°F), Gas Mark 4, for 25 minutes until tender and just beginning to brown, spooning the pan juices over the pears halfway through cooking and again at the end.

Spoon into shallow dishes, drizzle with the pan juices and serve with crème fraîche or Greek yogurt.

# BAKED HONEY, CARDAMOM & CINNAMON FIGS

*Serves:* 4

*Prep time:* 5 minutes

*Cook time:* 22 minutes

12 ripe fresh figs

1 tablespoon ghee or butter, plus extra for greasing

2 teaspoons cardamom seeds

2 cinnamon sticks

grated rind of 1 lemon

4–5 tablespoons clear honey

Greek yogurt, crème fraîche or clotted cream, to serve

icing (confectioners') sugar, for dusting

Cut each fig lengthways into quarters, keeping the base intact, and place in a lightly greased ovenproof dish.

Melt the ghee or butter in a small saucepan, stir in the cardamom seeds, cinnamon sticks, lemon rind and honey and cook for 2 minutes until bubbling. Pour the mixture evenly over the figs.

Bake in a preheated oven, 200°C (400°F), Gas Mark 6, for 20 minutes. Serve dusted with icing sugar accompanied by yogurt, crème fraîche or clotted cream dolloped into the centre of each fig.

# PAN-FRIED PEACH & PLUM CINNAMON CRUNCH

*Serves:* 4

*Prep time:* 10 minutes

*Cook time:* 10 minutes

75 g (3 oz) butter

4 peaches, halved, stoned (pitted) and cut into wedges

6 plums, halved and stoned (pitted)

4 tablespoons soft light brown sugar

1 teaspoon ground cinnamon

4 digestive biscuits (graham crackers), crushed

ice cream, to serve

Heat half the butter in a large, flameproof frying pan (skillet). Add the peaches, plums and sugar and simmer for 5 minutes, turning occasionally, until soft.

In a separate saucepan, melt the remaining butter and stir in the cinnamon. Add the crushed biscuits and stir to coat. Sprinkle over the peaches and plums.

Place the frying pan under a medium grill (broiler) and cook for 5 minutes until golden and crunchy. Serve with ice cream.

*Makes:* 8
*Prep time:* 30 minutes
*Cook time:* 1–1¼ hours

# Banoffee Meringues

3 egg whites

100 g (3½ oz) light muscovado (brown) sugar

75 g (3 oz) caster (superfine) sugar

## TO SERVE

1 small ripe banana

1 tablespoon lemon juice

150 ml (¼ pint) double (heavy) cream

8 tablespoons ready-made toffee fudge ice cream sauce

Whisk the egg whites in a large clean bowl until stiff. Gradually whisk in the sugars, a teaspoonful at a time, until it has all been added. Whisk for a few minutes more until the meringue mixture is thick and glossy.

Using a dessert spoon, take a large scoop of meringue mixture. Scoop it off the first spoon using a second spoon and drop onto a large baking sheet lined with nonstick baking paper to make an oval-shaped meringue. Repeat the process to make 16 meringues.

Bake in a preheated oven, 110°C (225°F), Gas Mark ¼ , for 1–1¼ hours or until the meringues are firm and may be easily peeled off the paper. Leave to cool still on the paper.

To serve, roughly mash the banana with the lemon juice. Whip the cream until it forms soft peaks, then whisk in 2 tablespoons of the toffee fudge sauce. Combine with the mashed banana, then use to sandwich the meringues together in pairs. Drizzle with the remaining toffee fudge sauce and serve immediately. Unfilled meringues may be stored in an airtight tin for up to 3 days.

# STICKY TOFFEE APPLES

***Serves:*** **4**
***Prep time:*** **10 minutes**
***Cook time:*** **30 minutes, plus cooling**

100 g (3½ oz) butter

1 tablespoon soft dark brown sugar

1 teaspoon lemon juice

3 dessert apples, peeled, cored and cut into 8 slices each

8 sheets of filo pastry (about 45 x 25 cm / 18 x 10 inches)

## FOR THE TOFFEE SAUCE

25 g (1 oz) butter

65 g (2½ oz) soft dark brown sugar

50 ml (2 fl oz) double (heavy) cream

Line a baking sheet with baking paper. Melt half the butter in a frying pan (skillet) with the sugar and lemon juice. Add the apples and cook for 8–10 minutes. Meanwhile, melt the remaining butter and brush over 4 sheets of filo pastry.

Top each buttered side with a second sheet of pastry. Brush again with butter and fold each double layer in half lengthways to form 4 rectangles.

Remove the apples from the pan, reserving the juices. Divide the apples between the sheets of pastry, arranging them at one end. Fold the other end of the pastry over the top to cover the apples. Turn in the edges and roll them over to create 4 parcels, then arrange on a baking sheet. Bake in a preheated oven, 180°C (350°F), Gas Mark 4, for 12–15 minutes.

Meanwhile, make the toffee sauce. Put the butter, sugar and cream in the frying pan. Stir over a low heat until the sugar has melted, then bubble for 1–2 minutes until thick and deep golden. Remove from the heat and cool. Remove the apple parcels from the oven and serve drizzled with the toffee sauce.

# Chocolate Bread & Butter Pudding

*Serves:* 4
*Prep time:* 20 minutes, plus standing
*Cook time:* 25 minutes

4 chocolate croissants
50 g (2 oz) unsalted butter
50 g (2 oz) caster (superfine) sugar
¼ teaspoon ground mixed spice
300 ml (½ pint) milk
4 eggs
1 teaspoon vanilla extract
icing (confectioners') sugar, to decorate
pouring cream or chocolate sauce (see page 26), to serve

Grease a 1.2 litre (2 pint) shallow, round, ovenproof pie dish. Slice the croissants thickly and spread the butter over one side of each cut face of croissant. Stand the croissant slices upright and close together in the dish to completely fill it.

Mix the sugar and spice together, then sprinkle over the croissants and between the gaps. Stand the dish in a large roasting tin.

Beat the milk, eggs and vanilla extract together, then strain into the dish. Leave to stand for 15 minutes.

Pour hot water from the tap into the roasting tin to come halfway up the sides of the pie dish. Bake in a preheated oven, 180°C (350°F), Gas Mark 4, for about 25 minutes until the pudding is golden and the custard just set.

Lift the dish out of the roasting tin, dust with sifted icing sugar and serve the pudding warm with a little pouring cream or chocolate sauce.

# STEAMED PUDDINGS WITH GOLDEN SYRUP

(VG)

*Serves:* **4**
*Prep time:* **15 minutes**
*Cook time:* **1½ minutes**

vegan margarine, for greasing
6 tablespoons golden syrup
75 g (3 oz) caster (superfine) sugar
75 g (3 oz) vegetable oil
150 g (5 oz) self-raising flour
125 ml (4 fl oz) dairy-free milk
½ tablespoon apple cider vinegar or white wine vinegar
1 teaspoon baking powder
pinch of salt

Grease 4 microwave-safe pudding moulds (approximately 150 ml/¼ pint in size) well with margarine. Divide the golden syrup between the moulds and set aside.

In a separate bowl, mix together all the remaining ingredients, then divide between the moulds.

Cover the pudding moulds with clingfilm (plastic wrap) and microwave one at a time on high for 1 minute 30 seconds. Leave to stand for 5 minutes before turning out onto a plate – it can help to loosen the edges with a knife first.

For another flavour option, try replacing the golden syrup with marmalade or jam (jelly).

# CARAMEL & BANANA BREAD PUDDING

*Serves:* **6**
*Prep time:* **15 minutes, plus soaking**
*Cook time:* **50–60 minutes**

50 g (2 oz) butter, softened
8 slices of brioche bread
6 tablespoons dulce de leche or thick caramel sauce
2 bananas
300 ml (½ pint) milk
300 ml (½ pint) double (heavy) cream
3 eggs
1 teaspoon ground cinnamon
25 g (1 oz) caster (superfine) sugar

Butter the brioche on both sides, then spread 4 tablespoons of the dulce de leche or caramel sauce over 4 of the slices. Top each with another slice of bread. Cut into rough squares and arrange in a greased 1.2 litre (2 pint) baking dish. Slice 1 of the bananas and scatter over the brioche.

Mash the remaining banana in a bowl, add the remaining ingredients and whisk together. Pour over the bread and leave to soak for 30 minutes.

Dot the remaining dulce de leche or caramel sauce over the top of the pudding. Bake in a preheated oven, 160°C (325°F), Gas Mark 3, for 50–60 minutes until puffed and just cooked through.

# STICKY TOFFEE PUDDINGS

*Serves:* 8
*Prep time:* 20 minutes
*Cook time:* 45–50 minutes

- 125 g (4 oz) stoned (pitted) dates, chopped
- 150 ml (¼ pint) of cold water
- 125 g (4 oz) butter, softened, plus extra for greasing
- 125 g (4 oz) caster (superfine) sugar
- 1 teaspoon vanilla extract
- 3 eggs
- 175 g (6 oz) self-raising flour
- 1 teaspoon baking powder
- ice cream, to serve (optional)

### FOR THE TOFFEE SAUCE

- 300 ml (½ pint) double (heavy) cream, plus extra to serve
- 125 g (4 oz) light brown sugar
- 50 g (2 oz) unsalted butter

Put the dates in a small saucepan with the measurement water and simmer for 5 minutes until the dates are soft and pulpy. Blend to a purée, then allow to cool.

Make the sauce. Heat half the cream in a small, heavy-bottomed pan with the sugar and butter until the sugar dissolves. Bring to the boil, then let the sauce bubble for about 5 minutes until a rich, dark caramel. Stir in the remaining cream and set aside.

Grease 8 x 200 ml (7 fl oz) pudding moulds and line the bottoms with nonstick baking paper. Beat the butter, sugar, vanilla extract, eggs, flour and baking powder in a bowl for 1–2 minutes until pale and creamy. Stir the date purée into the pudding mixture.

Divide the mixture between the moulds. Level the tops and place in a roasting tin. Pour boiling water to a depth of 1.5 cm (¾ inch) in the tin and cover with foil. Bake in a preheated oven, 180°C (350°F), Gas Mark 4, for 35–40 minutes, or until risen and firm to the touch.

Leave the puddings in the moulds while you reheat the sauce, then loosen the edges of the moulds, invert the puddings onto serving plates and peel off the paper. Top with the sauce and serve with extra cream or ice cream.

# GINGER & TREACLE SPONGE PUDDING

*Serves:* 4
*Prep time:* **5 minutes**
*Cook time:* **25 minutes**

175 g (6 oz) golden syrup
125 g (4 oz) butter or margarine, plus extra for greasing
125 g (4 oz) caster (superfine) sugar
2 eggs
125 g (4 oz) self-raising flour
1½ teaspoons ground ginger
single (light) cream or custard, to serve

Grease an 1.2 litre (2 pint) ovenproof dish and pour in the golden syrup.

Place all remaining ingredients in a bowl and beat until smooth, then pour the mixture over the golden syrup. Smooth the mixture with a spatula to make an even layer. Bake in the preheated oven, 180°C (350°F), Gas Mark 4, for 20–25 minutes until risen and golden.

Serve drizzled with cream or warm custard.

# SPICY FRUIT BREAD PUDDINGS

*Serves:* 4
*Prep time:* **5 minutes**
*Cook time:* **28 minutes**

25 g (1 oz) chilled butter, grated, plus extra for greasing
150 g (5 oz) wholemeal (whole-wheat) bread
150 ml (¼ pint) milk
30 g (1 oz) sultanas
50 g (2 oz) dried apricots, diced
50 g (2 oz) blueberries
50 g (2 oz) dark muscovado (brown) sugar
½ teaspoon mixed spice
1 teaspoon sunflower seeds
1 teaspoon pumpkin seeds
1 egg, beaten
natural (plain) yogurt or crème fraîche, to serve (optional)

Lightly grease 4 ramekins. Break the bread into small chunks and place in a large bowl. Pour over the milk and leave to soak for 10–12 minutes.

Add the remaining ingredients and mix well. Spoon into the prepared ramekins. Bake in a preheated oven, 180°C (350°F), Gas Mark 4, for 12–15 minutes until just golden.

Serve immediately with natural yogurt or crème fraîche, if liked.

# CHOCOLATE PUDDLE PUDDING

*Serves:* 4–6
*Prep time:* 15 minutes
*Cook time:* 15 minutes

75 g (3 oz) butter, at room temperature

75 g (3 oz) light soft brown sugar

3 eggs

65 g (2½ oz) self-raising flour

3 tablespoons cocoa powder

½ teaspoon baking powder

icing (confectioners') sugar, to decorate

vanilla ice cream, to serve

### FOR THE SAUCE

2 tablespoons cocoa powder

50 g (2 oz) light soft brown sugar

250 ml (8 fl oz) boiling water

Rub a little of the butter all over the base and sides of a cooking dish and stand the dish on a baking sheet. Put the butter, sugar and eggs in a large bowl and sift in the flour, cocoa powder and baking powder. Beat together with a wooden spoon until they form a smooth mixture. Spoon the pudding mixture into the prepared dish and spread the top level.

Make the sauce. Put the cocoa powder and sugar into a small bowl and mix in a little of the measurement boiling water to make a smooth paste. Gradually mix in the rest of the water, then pour the cocoa sauce over the pudding mixture.

Bake in a preheated oven, 180°C (350°F), Gas Mark 4, for 15 minutes, or until the sauce has sunk to the bottom of the dish and the pudding is well risen. Sift a little icing sugar over the pudding and serve with vanilla ice cream or a little cream.

# STEAMED APPLE PUDDING

*Serves:* 4
*Prep time:* 20 minutes
*Cook time:* 2 hours

- 125 g (4 oz) unsalted butter, plus extra for greasing
- 4 tablespoons golden syrup
- 2 cooking apples (about 500 g / 1 lb), peeled and cored
- 100 g (3½ oz) caster (superfine) sugar
- 2 eggs, beaten
- 200 g (7 oz) self-raising flour
- grated rind of 1 orange, and 3 tablespoons of the juice

Grease a 1.2 litre (2 pint) pudding basin lightly and line the base with a circle of nonstick baking paper. Spoon in the golden syrup, then thickly slice 1 apple and arrange in an even layer on top. Coarsely grate the remaining apple.

Cream the butter and sugar in a bowl until pale and creamy. Gradually mix in alternate spoonfuls of beaten egg and flour until both have all been added and the mixture is smooth.

Stir in the grated apple, orange rind and juice, then spoon into the pudding basin. Level the surface and cover with a piece of pleated nonstick baking paper and foil. Tie in place with string, adding a string handle.

Lower the basin into the top of a steamer set over a saucepan of simmering water, cover with a lid and steam for 2 hours until the pudding is well risen and a knife comes out clean when inserted into the centre of the sponge.

Remove the foil and paper, loosen the edge of the pudding and turn out onto a plate with a rim. Serve immediately with custard or vanilla ice cream.

# ORANGE & CINNAMON PUDDINGS

*Serves:* 4

*Prep time:* 10 minutes

*Cook time:* 25 minutes

100 g (3½ oz) butter, softened, plus extra for greasing

4 tablespoons golden syrup, plus extra, to serve

2 large oranges

100 g (3½ oz) soft brown sugar

150 g (5 oz) self-raising flour

½ teaspoon ground cinnamon

2 eggs

Grease 4 x 200 ml (7 fl oz) pudding moulds or ramekins and divide the golden syrup between them. Finely grate the rind of both oranges and place in a food processor, then use a sharp knife to remove the pith. Thickly slice 1 orange. Carefully arrange 1 orange slice at the bottom of each mould. Chop the remaining orange flesh, removing any pith or seeds, and place in the food processor together with the remaining ingredients. Whizz to make a smooth batter.

Spoon the batter into the moulds. Place in a roasting tin half-filled with boiling water and cover with kitchen foil. Bake in a preheated oven, 180°C (350°F), Gas Mark 4, for 20–25 minutes until just cooked through. Leave for 1 minute in the moulds, then turn out onto plates and serve with a little more golden syrup drizzled over, if liked.

# MAPLE SYRUP, DATE & PECAN PUDDINGS

*Serves:* 6

*Prep time:* 10 minutes

*Cook time:* 30 minutes

150 g (5 oz) unsalted butter, diced, plus extra for greasing

175 g (6 oz) ready-to-eat pitted dates

50 ml (2 fl oz) maple syrup, plus 6 teaspoons

3 eggs, beaten

175 g (6 oz) self-raising flour

50 g (2 oz) pecan nuts, chopped

custard, to serve

Lightly grease 6 x 150 ml (¼ pint) metal pudding moulds and place on a baking sheet. Put the dates and 200 ml (7 fl oz) of cold water in a small saucepan and bring to the boil, then cover and simmer for 5–6 minutes. Transfer to a large bowl and mash the dates with the back of a spoon or fork.

Put the butter and the 50 ml (2 fl oz) of maple syrup in the saucepan and stir until the butter has melted, then gently stir in the eggs, flour and pecans.

Place 1 teaspoonful of maple syrup in each of the prepared pudding moulds and spoon in the sponge mixture. Bake in a preheated oven, 180°C (350°F), Gas Mark 4, for 20 minutes, or until risen and firm to the touch. Leave to cool in the moulds for a few minutes.

Turn the puddings out into bowls and serve with custard.

*Serves:* 6
*Prep time:* 10 minutes
*Cook time:* 20 minutes

# Caramel Chocolate Fondants

- 200 g (7 oz) unsalted butter, plus extra for greasing
- 225 g (7½ oz) plain dark chocolate, broken into small pieces
- 50 g (2 oz) plain (all-purpose) flour, plus extra for dusting
- 3 large eggs, plus 2 large egg yolks
- 75 g (3 oz) soft light brown sugar
- 6 dessertspoons dulce de leche or thick caramel sauce
- vanilla ice cream, to serve

Place the butter and chocolate in a small saucepan over a low heat and warm until just melted. Stir gently, then set aside.

Meanwhile, grease 6 x 200 ml (7 fl oz) freezer-proof and heatproof ramekins or metal pudding moulds with butter and dust lightly with flour, then place on a baking sheet.

Place the eggs plus egg yolks and sugar in a large bowl and beat with a hand-held electric whisk until thick and creamy. Fold in the flour and melted chocolate.

Spoon the mixture into the prepared ramekins and dollop 1 spoonful of the dulce de leche or caramel sauce into the centre of each one, then cover with a little of the chocolate mixture. Place in the freezer for 8–10 minutes.

Remove from the freezer. Bake in a preheated oven, 200°C (400°F), Gas Mark 6, for 12–14 minutes until almost firm but still with a slight wobble in the centre. Leave to cool in the dishes for 2 minutes, then invert onto serving dishes and serve each with vanilla ice cream.

# HOT BLACKBERRY & APPLE TRIFLE

*Serves:* 4
*Prep time:* 20 minutes, plus cooling
*Cook time:* 20–25 minutes

150 g (5 oz) fresh or frozen blackberries

2 dessert apples, unpeeled, cored and sliced

1 tablespoon water

50 g (2 oz) caster (superfine) sugar

4 trifle sponges

3 tablespoons dry or sweet sherry

425 g (14 oz) can or carton custard

### FOR THE MERINGUE

3 egg whites

75 g (3 oz) caster (superfine) sugar

Put the blackberries, apples, measurement water and sugar in a saucepan, then cover and simmer for 5 minutes, or until the fruit has softened. Leave the mixture to cool slightly.

Break the trifle sponges into chunks and arrange in an even layer in the base of a 1.2 litre (2 pint) ovenproof pie or soufflé dish and drizzle with the sherry. Spoon the poached fruit and syrup over the top, then cover with the custard.

Make the meringue. Whisk the egg whites in a large, dry bowl until stiffly peaking, then gradually whisk in the sugar, a teaspoonful at a time, until the meringue is stiff and glossy. Spoon over the custard and swirl the top with the back of a spoon.

Bake in a preheated oven, 180°C (350°F), Gas Mark 4, for 15–20 minutes until heated through and the meringue is golden. Serve immediately.

# CARAMEL ICE CREAM CAKE

*Serves:* 8–10

*Prep time:* **10 minutes, plus standing, chilling and freezing**

1 litre (1¾ pints) good-quality vanilla ice cream

250 g (8 oz) digestive biscuits (graham crackers), crushed

75 g (3 oz) butter, melted

200 g (7 oz) shop-bought soft butterscotch fudge

2 tablespoons single (light) cream

Remove the ice cream from the freezer and leave to stand at room temperature for 30–45 minutes until it is well softened.

Meanwhile, put the crushed biscuits in a bowl, add the melted butter and mix together until the biscuits are moistened. Press the biscuit mixture into a 23 cm (9 inch) round springform tin, pressing it so it forms a 2.5 cm (1 inch) border up the side of the tin. Chill in the refrigerator for 20 minutes.

Put the fudge and cream in a saucepan and heat gently, stirring, until the fudge has melted. Carefully spread two-thirds of the fudge mixture over the biscuit case. Spoon the ice cream over the top and level the surface.

Drizzle the remaining caramel over the ice cream with a spoon and freeze for 4 hours. Unmould the cake and serve in wedges.

# CINNAMON-SPICED CHERRIES

*Serves:* 4

*Cook time:* **10 minutes**

25 g (1 oz) caster (superfine) sugar

350 ml (12 fl oz) rosé wine

strip of pared lemon rind

1 cinnamon stick

500 g (1 lb) cherries, pitted if liked

Combine all the ingredients in a saucepan. Bring to the boil, then reduce the heat and simmer for 5 minutes until the sugar has dissolved and the cherries are tender.

Use a slotted spoon to transfer the cherries to a serving dish, then cook the liquid over a high heat for 3–4 minutes until syrupy. Remove the cinnamon stick and lemon rind, then pour over the cherries and serve warm or cold. The perfect accompaniment to vanilla ice cream.

# Chocolate & Pistachio Soufflés

*Serves:* 6
*Prep time:* 10 minutes
*Cook time:* 30 minutes

butter, for greasing

25 g (1 oz) pistachio nuts, ground

150 g (5 oz) plain dark chocolate (72% cocoa solids), broken into small pieces

4 eggs, separated

100 g (3½ oz) caster (superfine) sugar

2 teaspoons cornflour (cornstarch)

cocoa powder or icing (confectioners') sugar, for dusting (optional)

Grease 6 x 175 ml (6 fl oz) ramekins, then lightly dust with 1 tablespoon of the ground pistachios to cover the base and sides. (This will help the soufflés to rise.) Place on a baking sheet.

Melt the chocolate in a heatproof bowl set over a saucepan of gently simmering water, then leave to cool slightly.

Meanwhile, whisk the egg whites in a clean large bowl with a hand-held electric whisk until stiff, then gradually whisk in half the sugar until the mixture is thick and glossy.

Stir the remaining sugar, egg yolks and cornflour into the cooled chocolate mixture. Gently fold some of the egg white mixture into the chocolate mixture, then gently fold in the remainder, with the remaining pistachios. Spoon into the prepared ramekins and spread the tops level, then clean the edges.

Bake in a preheated oven, 190°C (375°F), Gas Mark 5, for 20 minutes, or until risen. Dust with cocoa powder or icing sugar (if using) and serve immediately.

# Orange, Rhubarb & Ginger Slump

*Serves:* 6
*Prep time:* 10 minutes
*Cook time:* 20–25 minutes

- 750 g (1½ lb) rhubarb, chopped into 1.5 cm (¾ inch) pieces
- ½ teaspoon ground ginger
- grated rind and juice of 1 orange
- 50 g (2 oz) golden caster (superfine) sugar
- 4 tablespoons mascarpone cheese
- 175 g (6 oz) self-raising flour, sifted
- 50 g (2 oz) unsalted butter, cut into small pieces
- grated rind of ½ lemon
- 6 tablespoons milk
- custard, to serve (optional)

Put the rhubarb, ginger, orange rind and juice and half the sugar in a saucepan. Bring to boil, then reduce the heat and simmer for about 5–6 minutes until the rhubarb is just tender.

Transfer the rhubarb to an ovenproof dish and spoon over dollops of mascarpone.

Place the flour in a bowl. Add the butter and rub in with your fingertips until the mixture resembles fine breadcrumbs. Stir through the remaining sugar, the lemon rind and milk until combined. Place spoonfuls of the mixture over the rhubarb and mascarpone.

Bake in a preheated oven, 200°C (400°F), Gas Mark 6, for 12–15 minutes until golden and bubbling. Serve with custard, if liked.

# Caramel Apple Crumble

*Serves:* 4
*Prep time:* 15 minutes
*Cook time:* 25 minutes

spray oil, for greasing

750 g (1½ lb) Bramley cooking apples, cored, peeled and thickly sliced

75 g (3 oz) butter, plus extra for greasing

3 tablespoons soft light brown sugar

6 whole cloves

50 g (2 oz) sultanas

75ml (3 fl oz) cold water

## For the crumble topping

75 g (3 oz) rolled oats

75 g (3 oz) plain (all-purpose) flour

50 g (2 oz) ground hazelnuts

50 g (2 oz) soft light brown sugar

2 teaspoons ground cinnamon

100 g (3½ oz) butter, diced

ice cream or cream, to serve (optional)

Lightly oil 4 x 300 ml (½ pint) baking dishes with spray oil. Put the apples in a saucepan with the butter, sugar, cloves, sultanas and measurement water. Cover and cook over a low heat for 5–6 minutes until the apples are just softened. Divide between the prepared dishes.

Make the crumble topping. Put all the dry ingredients in a bowl and stir well until combined. Add the butter and rub in with your fingertips until the mixture resembles coarse breadcrumbs. Spoon the crumble topping over the apple mixture.

Bake in a preheated oven, 190°C (375°F), Gas Mark 5, for 25 minutes until bubbling and golden. Serve warm with ice cream or cream, if liked.

# Chocolate Cream Pie

*Serves:* 6–8
*Prep time:* 45 minutes, plus chilling and cooling
*Cook time:* 50 minutes

235 g (7 ½ oz) plain (all-purpose) flour

15 g (½ oz) cocoa powder

pinch of salt

125 g (4 oz) butter, diced

2½–3 tablespoons cold water

flour, for dusting

### FOR THE FILLING

150 g (5 oz) plain dark chocolate, broken into pieces

500 g (1lb) cream cheese, softened

100 g (3½ oz) caster (superfine) sugar

1 tablespoon plain (all-purpose) flour

1 teaspoon vanilla extract

3 eggs

Add the flour, cocoa powder, salt and butter to a large mixing bowl. Rub together with your fingertips until the mixture resembles fine crumbs. Gradually mix in just enough water to enable the crumbs to be squeezed together to form a soft but not sticky dough. Knead very lightly until smooth.

Roll the dough out on a lightly floured surface a little larger than a greased 23 cm (9 inch) fluted loose-bottomed tart tin 3.5 cm (1½ inches) deep. Press the pastry over the base and sides and trim off the excess so it stands just above the top of the tin. Prick the base with a fork, then chill for 15 minutes. Line the tart case with nonstick baking paper and add baking beans. Bake blind in a preheated oven, 190°C (375°F), Gas Mark 5 for 15 minutes. Remove the paper and baking beans and bake for a further 5 minutes. Remove from the oven and reduce the oven temperature to 150°C (300°F), Gas Mark 2.

Make the filling. Melt the chocolate in a bowl over a pan of hot water. The put the cream cheese in a bowl, add the sugar, flour and vanilla extract, then gradually beat in the eggs until smooth. Ladle about one-third into the chocolate bowl and mix until smooth.

Pour the cheese mixture into the tart case, then pipe the chocolate mixture over the top and swirl together with the handle of a teaspoon for a marbled effect. Bake for 30 minutes until set around the edges, beginning to crack and the centre still wobbles slightly. Leave to cool in the turned-off oven. When cool, refrigerate overnight. Remove the pie from the tin, place on a plate and slice to serve.

# APRICOT & BLUEBERRY COBBLER

*Serves:* 4
*Prep time:* 10 minutes
*Cook time:* 20 minutes

12 ripe apricots, halved and stoned (pitted)
150 g (5 oz) blueberries
2 tablespoons light muscovado (brown) sugar
175 g (6 oz) self-raising flour, plus extra for dusting
50 g (2 oz) unsalted butter, diced
50 g (2 oz) caster (superfine) sugar
125 ml (4 fl oz) buttermilk
milk, for brushing

Place the apricots and blueberries in a 750 ml (1¼ pint) ovenproof dish and sprinkle over the muscovado sugar.

Place the flour in a bowl, add the butter and rub in with the fingertips until the mixture resembles fine breadcrumbs. Stir in the caster sugar, then add the buttermilk a little at a time, to form a slightly sticky, soft dough.

Turn the dough out onto a lightly floured surface and pat out until it is 1 cm (½ inch) thick. Cut out 8 rounds using a 6 cm (2½ inch) cutter.

Arrange over the top of the fruit and brush with a little milk. Bake in a preheated oven, 180°C (350°F), Gas Mark 4, for 20 minutes or until the scones are golden and the fruit is bubbling. Serve immediately.

# CARAMELIZED BERRY RICE PUDDING

*Serves:* 2
*Prep time:* 5 minutes
*Cook time:* 10 minutes

125 g (4 oz) frozen mixed summer berries
1 tablespoon caster (superfine) sugar
425 g (14 oz) can rice pudding
4 tablespoons natural (plain) yogurt
1 tablespoon soft light brown sugar

Place the fruit in a saucepan with the caster sugar and heat, stirring, for 3–4 minutes until the fruit has softened and defrosted. Tip the fruit and juice into flameproof dishes.

Mix together the rice pudding and yogurt in a bowl, then spoon over the fruit. Sprinkle over the brown sugar and place under a preheated hot grill (broiler) for about 2 minutes until the sugar starts to melt and caramelize. Cool slightly before serving.

# Banoffee Pie

*Serves:* 6
*Prep time:* 25 minutes, plus chilling
*Cook time:* 4–5 minutes

150 g (5 oz) Rich Tea biscuits
65 g (2½ oz) butter
1 tablespoon golden syrup
300 ml (½ pint) double (heavy) cream
2 bananas
juice of ½ lemon

### FOR THE TOFFEE FILLING

100 g (3½ oz) butter
100 g (3½ oz) dark muscovado (brown) sugar
400 g (13 oz) can condensed milk

### TO DECORATE

diced toffees
grated chocolate (optional)

Crush the biscuits in a plastic food bag using a rolling pin. Melt the butter in a saucepan with the golden syrup, take off the heat and stir in the biscuit crumbs. Tip into an unbuttered 20 cm (8 inch) fluted loose-bottomed tart tin, then press over the base and up the sides with the back of a spoon into an even layer. Chill for 30 minutes.

Make the toffee filling. Melt the butter in a clean dry pan with the sugar. Add the condensed milk and stir well, then bring to the boil and cook over a medium heat for 4–5 minutes, stirring constantly, until the mixture begins to thicken, smells of toffee and crystallizes around the edges. Be careful not to overheat as the milk can scorch easily.

Pour the toffee into the pie case, leave to cool, then chill for 3½–4½ hours, or until ready to serve.

Whip the cream until it forms soft peaks. Slice the bananas and toss with the lemon juice, then fold into the cream and spoon over the pie. Decorate the top with diced toffees and grated chocolate, if liked. Serve within 2 hours of decorating.

# Baked Chocolate Cheesecake

*Serves:* 2
*Prep time:* 10 minutes, plus cooling
*Cook time:* 45 minutes

25 g (1 oz) unsalted butter, melted

75 g (3 oz) ratafia or ameretti biscuits, crushed

150 g (5 oz) cream cheese

25 g (1 oz) caster (superfine) sugar

50 g (2 oz) mascarpone

50 g (2 oz) dark plain chocolate, melted

1 egg

1 egg yolk

**TO DECORATE**

crème fraîche

chocolate shavings

Melt the butter in a saucepan. Add the crushed biscuits and mix well. Divide the mixture between two 10 cm (4 inch) tart tins, and press down to form the cheesecake bases.

Place the cream cheese, sugar, mascarpone and chocolate in a small pan and warm over a gentle heat, stirring until the mixture is melted and blended.

Remove from the heat, allow to cool and then beat in the egg and the yolk.

Divide the chocolate mixture between the tart tins and place them on a baking sheet. Bake in a preheated oven, 180°C (350°F), Gas Mark 4, for 45 minutes, or until set. Remove from the oven and leave the cheesecakes to cool before transferring them to the refrigerator. Chill until required, then decorate with a dollop of crème fraîche and chocolate shavings.

# PEACHY CINNAMON CHEESECAKE

*Serves:* 6

*Prep time:* **20 minutes, plus chilling**

250 g (8 oz) digestive biscuits (graham crackers), crushed

1 teaspoon ground cinnamon

125 g (4 oz) butter, melted

400 g (13 oz) cream cheese

120 g (3¾ oz) peach yogurt

100 g (3½ oz) icing (confectioners') sugar, sifted

410–420 g (13⅓–13¾ oz) can peach halves in light syrup, drained and sliced

In a large bowl, mix the biscuit crumbs with half the cinnamon and the butter until well coated, then press the mixture into a 23 cm (9 inch) tart or cake tin (cake pan). Chill in the refrigerator until required.

Meanwhile, place the cream cheese and yogurt in a bowl and beat in the icing sugar and remaining cinnamon until smooth and thick. Spoon the mixture over the base and smooth down evenly. Return to the refrigerator and chill for at least 20 minutes.

Cut and serve with the sliced peaches.

# NECTARINE BRÛLÉE

*Serves:* 6

*Prep time:* **10 minutes**

*Cook time:* **10–15 minutes**

500 g (1 lb) nectarines, stoned (pitted) and sliced

4 tablespoons orange liqueur, plus extra to flavour the fruit

350 ml (12 fl oz) soured cream

pinch of freshly grated nutmeg

1 teaspoon vanilla extract

125 g (4 oz) soft light brown sugar

brandy snaps, langues de chat or amaretti biscuits (cookies), to serve

Put the nectarines in a saucepan and add enough water to cover. Poach over a low heat for 5–10 minutes, or until tender. Drain and divide between 6 ramekins. Stir in a little orange liqueur.

Beat together the soured cream, nutmeg, vanilla extract and the measurement orange liqueur in a bowl until well combined. Spoon over the nectarine slices, then scatter the sugar over the top in a thick layer.

Cook under a preheated high grill (broiler until the sugar caramelizes. Serve with brandy snaps, langues de chat or amaretti.

# Vanilla Crème Brûlée

*Serves:* 6

*Prep time:* 20 minutes, plus standing and chilling

*Cook time:* 25–30 minutes

- 1 vanilla pod
- 600 ml (1 pint) double (heavy) cream
- 8 egg yolks
- 65 g (2½ oz) caster (superfine) sugar
- 3 tablespoons icing (confectioners') sugar

Slit the vanilla pod lengthways and place it in a saucepan. Pour the cream into the pan, then bring almost to the boil. Take off the heat and allow to stand for 15 minutes. Lift the pod out of the cream and, holding it against the side of the saucepan, scrape the black seeds into the cream. Discard the rest of the pod.

Use a fork to mix together the egg yolks and caster sugar in a bowl. Reheat the cream, then gradually mix it into the eggs and sugar. Strain the mixture back into the saucepan.

Place 6 ovenproof ramekins in a roasting tin, then divide the custard between them. Pour warm water around the dishes to come halfway up the sides. Bake in a preheated oven, 180°C (350°F), Gas Mark 4, for 20–25 minutes until the custard is just set with a slight softness at the centre.

Leave the dishes to cool in the water, then lift them out and chill in the refrigerator for 3–4 hours. About 25 minutes before serving, sprinkle with the icing sugar and caramelize using a blowtorch (or under a hot grill or broiler), then leave at room temperature.

# Amaretti & Chocolate Custard

*Serves:* 4
*Prep time:* 20 minutes, plus chilling
*Cook time:* 55–65 minutes

- 175 g (6 oz) granulated sugar
- 125 ml (4 fl oz) cold water
- 2 tablespoons cocoa powder
- 4 tablespoons boiling water
- 2 eggs
- 2 egg yolks
- 65 g (2½ oz) amaretti biscuits (cookies), finely crushed
- 450 ml (¾ pint) milk
- 150 ml (¼ pint) strong black coffee
- chocolate curls or a few amaretti biscuits (cookies), crumbled, to decorate

In a small saucepan, dissolve 125 g (4 oz) of the sugar in the measurement cold water, stirring occasionally, then increase the heat and boil for 5 minutes without stirring until golden brown, keeping a watchful eye towards the end of the cooking time.

Mix the cocoa powder with 2 tablespoons of the boiling water in a bowl. Mix the remaining sugar with the eggs, egg yolks and biscuits in a separate bowl.

Take the syrup off the heat as soon as it caramelizes. Add the remaining boiling water and tilt to mix. Pour into a 900 ml (1½ pint) ovenproof dish. Tilt to coat the base and halfway up the sides. Stand in a roasting tin.

Pour the milk into the drained caramel pan and bring just to the boil. Stir the cocoa mix into the egg mixture, then gradually whisk in the hot milk, followed by the coffee. Slowly pour into the caramel-lined dish.

Fill the roasting tin with hot water halfway up the sides of the dish. Bake in a preheated oven, 160°C (325°F), Gas Mark 3, for 50–60 minutes until the custard has just set but still wobbles slightly in the centre.

Take dish out of the tin, leave to cool, then chill for 4–5 hours or overnight. To turn out, stand in just-boiled water for 10 seconds, then invert on a plate. Decorate with chocolate curls or crumbled amaretti.

# CHOCOLATE & CARDAMOM POTS

*Serves:* 4
*Prep time:* 10 minutes
*Cook time:* 8 minutes

200 g (7 oz) good-quality dark chocolate, broken into squares
seeds from 8–10 cardamom pods, crushed
2 tablespoons coffee liqueur
2 tablespoons extra virgin olive oil
3 large eggs, separated
4 tablespoons whipped double (heavy) cream
cocoa powder, for dusting

Place the chocolate in a small, heatproof bowl with the cardamom, coffee liqueur and oil and set over a pan of barely simmering water. Leave the chocolate to melt very slowly without stirring for about 8 minutes.

Remove the bowl from the heat and quickly beat in the egg yolks. Set aside while you put the egg whites in a large bowl and whisk until stiff. Stir 1 tablespoon of the beaten whites into the chocolate mixture to slacken it, then carefully fold in the remaining egg whites with a metal spoon.

Divide the mixture between 4 ramekins or pretty coffee cups. Cover and chill for 2 hours, or until required. Serve with a little whipped cream and a dusting of cocoa powder.

# WHITE CHOCOLATE & STRAWBERRY CHEESECAKE

*Serves:* 6–8
*Prep time:* 10 minutes, plus chilling
*Cook time:* 10 minutes

150 g (5 oz) digestive biscuits (graham crackers), crushed
75 g (3 oz) unsalted butter, melted
200 g (7 oz) white chocolate, broken into small pieces
500 g (1 lb) mascarpone
25 g (1 oz) icing (confectioners') sugar, sifted
200 g (7 oz) strawberries, hulled and sliced
white chocolate curls, to decorate

Stir the biscuits into the melted butter and press into the base of a 20 cm (8 inch) loose-bottomed round cake tin (cake pan). Chill while you make the filling.

Melt the chocolate in a heatproof bowl set over a saucepan of gently simmering water, stirring occasionally.

Place the mascarpone in a bowl and whisk in the icing sugar until smooth. Whisk in the chocolate, then spread the mixture over the cheesecake base.

Chill for 15 minutes, then arrange the strawberries over the top and decorate with the chocolate curls. Serve immediately or chill until ready to serve.

# SLOW COOKER CRÈME CARAMELS

*Serves:* 4
*Prep time:* 20 minutes, plus chilling
*Cook time:* 2½–3½ hours

butter, for greasing
125 g (4 oz) granulated sugar
2 tablespoons boiling water
2 eggs
3 egg yolks
400 g (13 oz) can condensed milk
125 ml (4 fl oz) semi-skimmed milk
grated rind of ½ small lemon

Preheat a slow cooker on low. Lightly butter 4 x 250 ml (8 fl oz) metal pudding moulds. Pour the sugar and 125 ml (4 fl oz) of cold water into a small saucepan and heat gently, stirring occasionally until the sugar has dissolved. Increase the heat and boil for 5 minutes, without stirring, until the syrup has turned golden, keeping a watchful eye as it cooks. Take off the heat and add the boiling water. Tilt the pan to mix, and when the bubbles have subsided pour into the moulds, tilting them so that the syrup coats the base and sides.

Put the whole eggs and egg yolks into a bowl and fork together. Pour the condensed and fresh milk into a saucepan, bring to the boil, then gradually beat into the egg mixture until smooth. Strain back into the pan, then stir in the lemon rind.

Pour the custard into the syrup-lined moulds and cover the top of each one with foil, then transfer the moulds into the slow cooker. Pour hot water around the moulds so that the water comes halfway up the sides, then cover with the lid. Cook on low for 2½–3½ hours, or until the custard is set with a slight wobble in the centre. Lift out of the slow cooker pot with a tea towel (cloth kitchen towel), cool, then chill in the refrigerator for 3–4 hours or overnight.

Dip the base of the moulds into boiling water for 10 seconds, loosen the top of the custard with a fingertip, then turn out onto rimmed plates.

# RICOTTA WITH WARM CINNAMON HONEY

*Serves:* 4

*Prep time:* **10 minutes, plus freezing**

*Cook time:* **5 minutes**

500 g (1 lb) ricotta

8 tablespoons clear honey

½ teaspoon ground cinnamon

handful of raspberries, to serve

Line 4 x 125 ml (4 fl oz) dariole moulds with clingfilm (plastic wrap). Press the ricotta into the moulds, then place in the freezer for 5 minutes.

Meanwhile, gently warm the honey and cinnamon in a small saucepan.

Remove the moulds from the freezer and invert onto plates. Remove the clingfilm and pour over the warm syrup. Serve with a scattering of raspberries.

# APPLE, MAPLE & PECAN FOOL

*Serves:* 4

*Prep time:* **10 minutes, plus cooling and chilling**

200 g (7 oz) good-quality apple sauce

1 Granny Smith apple, peeled and grated or finely chopped

200 ml (7 fl oz) double (heavy) cream

250 ml (8 fl oz) custard

3 tablespoons maple syrup

25 g (1 oz) pecan nuts, toasted and chopped

pecan biscuits (cookies), to serve

Put the apple sauce and apple in a small saucepan, cook for 5 minutes to soften, then place in metal bowl in the freezer for a few minutes to cool.

Whip the cream until soft peaks form, then stir in the custard. Swirl through the apple purée and maple syrup, then spoon into serving dishes. Top with the pecans and serve with pecan biscuits.

# Coffee Chocolate Bavarois

*Serves:* 10
*Prep time:* 45 minutes, plus freezing and chilling
*Cook time:* 10 minutes

- 1 litre (1¾ pints) single (light) cream
- 150 g (5 oz) plain dark chocolate, chopped
- 2 teaspoons cornflour (cornstarch)
- 150 g (5 oz) golden caster (superfine) sugar
- 8 egg yolks
- 25 g (1 oz) powdered gelatine
- 1 tablespoon fresh, very strong espresso coffee,
- 4 tablespoons coffee liqueur

Line a 1 kg (2 lb) loaf tin (loaf pan) with nonstick baking paper and place in the freezer to chill.

Heat half the cream gently in a pan. Add the chocolate and stir until melted. Remove from the heat.

Put half the cornflour, half the sugar and 4 egg yolks in a bowl. Put the remaining cornflour, sugar and yolks in a second bowl. Stir, then slowly whisk the chocolate cream into one bowl. Transfer to the pan and heat gently, stirring until slightly thickened and smooth. Whisk in half the powdered gelatine, then pour into a jug (pitcher).

Pour half the chocolate cream into the prepared loaf tin. Freeze uncovered, on a flat surface, for 45 minutes until just set.

Combine the remaining cream, espresso coffee and coffee liqueur in a pan over a low heat. Whisk this into the mixture in the second bowl, transfer to the pan and warm through. Add the rest of the gelatine and whisk together. Remove from the heat and pour into a jug.

Pour half the coffee cream over the set chocolate cream and refreeze for another 30 minutes, or until just set. Pour over the remaining chocolate cream and freeze for 20 minutes until just set, then pour on the final coffee cream layer. Chill for 4 hours. Run a knife around the sides, turn onto a board and slice to serve.

# CARAMEL & HONEYCOMB MOUSSE

*Serves:* 6
*Prep time:* 15 minutes, plus cooling and chilling
*Cook time:* 10–12 minutes

- 100 g (3½ oz) butter
- 50 g (2 oz) soft light brown sugar
- 397 g (13 oz) can condensed milk
- 150 g (5 oz) good-quality milk chocolate, broken into pieces
- 250 ml (8 fl oz) double (heavy) cream
- 40 g (1½ oz) bar of milk chocolate with golden honeycomb, roughly chopped, plus extra to decorate

To make the caramel, put the butter, sugar and condensed milk in a heavy-based saucepan, and heat over a low heat until the sugar has dissolved, then cook for 5 minutes, stirring continuously until just beginning to darken. Remove from the heat and leave to cool.

Melt the chocolate in a heatproof bowl set over a saucepan of simmering water, stirring occasionally, making sure that the water doesn't touch the base of the bowl. Leave to cool slightly.

Place the caramel in a bowl with the cream and whisk with a hand-held electric whisk until the mixture starts to thicken and leaves a trail.

Stir a little of the caramel mixture into the melted chocolate, then fold the chocolate mixture into the caramel mixture until well combined. Stir in the chocolate honeycomb.

Spoon into 6 small glasses and chill for 15–30 minutes (no longer, otherwise the honeycomb will start to dissolve). Decorate with a little extra chocolate honeycomb before serving.

# Chocolate & Gingernut Mousse

*Serves:* 4
*Prep time:* 25 minutes, plus chilling
*Cook time:* 10 minutes

200 g (7 oz) dark chocolate, broken into pieces

3 tablespoons strong coffee

3 eggs, separated

150 g (5 oz) gingernut biscuits (cookies)

40 g (1½ oz) butter

4 tablespoons crème fraîche

drinking chocolate, sifted, to decorate

Melt the chocolate in a bowl set over a saucepan of simmering water. Stir in the coffee, then gradually mix in the egg yolks one at a time. Leave to cool slightly.

Place the biscuits in a plastic food bag and crush with a rolling pin to make fine crumbs. Melt the butter in a small saucepan, then stir in the crumbs. Line 4 x 150 ml (¼ pint) ramekins with clingfilm (plastic wrap) so that the film overhangs the edges of the dishes. Divide half the crumbs between the ramekins and press flat.

Whisk the egg whites until soft peaks, then stir a spoonful into the chocolate mixture to loosen it slightly. Fold in the remaining egg whites using a metal spoon. Pour the mousse mixture into the ramekins, level the surfaces, then sprinkle with the remaining crumbs. Chill for 4–5 hours, or until set.

When ready to serve, lift the puddings out of the ramekins using the clingfilm, then peel the clingfilm away. Top each pudding with a spoonful of crème fraîche and decorate with a light dusting of drinking chocolate.

# Christmas Pudding Parfait with Butterscotch

*Serves:* 12
*Prep time:* 30 minutes, plus freezing
*Cook time:* 10 minutes

- finely grated rind and juice of 1 orange
- 2 tablespoons whisky liqueur or sherry, plus 12 teaspoons to serve
- 125 g (4 oz) raisins
- 125 g (4 oz) prunes, chopped
- 1 teaspoon ground mixed spice
- 125 g (4 oz) dark muscovado (brown) sugar, plus 1 tablespoon extra
- 4 large eggs, separated
- 575 ml (18 fl oz) double (heavy) cream, whipped until softly peaking
- 125 g (4 oz) plain dark chocolate flavoured with orange and spices, grated

## For the Butterscotch Sauce

- 50 g (2 oz) butter
- 50 g (2 oz) golden caster (superfine) sugar
- 75 g (3 oz) light muscovado (brown) sugar
- 150 g (5 oz) golden syrup
- 125 ml (4 fl oz) double (heavy) cream
- a few drops of vanilla extract
- juice of ½ lemon

Heat the orange rind and juice and whisky liqueur or sherry gently in a pan with the raisins, prunes and mixed spice for 3–5 minutes until the fruit has plumped up and the liquid has been absorbed. Purée in a food processor.

Beat 125 g (4 oz) sugar and the egg yolks together in a bowl for 5 minutes until thick and creamy. Fold in the cream. Add the blended fruit and chocolate.

Whisk the egg whites in a grease-free bowl until softly peaking. Whisk in the extra 1 tablespoon sugar. Fold the egg whites into the rest of the mixture and gently mix together.

Line a 1 kg (2 lb) loaf tin (loaf pan) with clingfilm (plastic wrap), then pour in the mixture and freeze in the tin for 6 hours.

Meanwhile, make the butterscotch sauce. Mix the butter, caster and muscovado sugars, and the golden syrup in a pan. Heat gently, stirring, until melted and smooth. Continue to cook over a low heat for 5 minutes. Remove from the heat and slowly stir in the cream, vanilla extract and the lemon juice. Set aside until ready to serve.

Serve the parfait sliced on plates drizzled with 1 teaspoon whisky liqueur or sherry around each slice, and the butterscotch sauce.

# CHERRY & CINNAMON ZABAGLIONE

*Serves:* 4
*Prep time:* 10 minutes
*Cook time:* 12–15 minutes

4 egg yolks
125 g (4 oz) caster (superfine) sugar
150 ml (¼ pint) cream sherry
large pinch of ground cinnamon
425 g (14 oz) can black cherries in syrup
2 amaretti biscuits (cookies), crumbled, to decorate

Pour 5 cm (2 inches) of water into a medium saucepan and bring to the boil. Cover with a large heatproof bowl, making sure that the water does not touch the base of the bowl. Reduce the heat so that the water is simmering, then add the egg yolks, sugar, sherry and cinnamon to the bowl. Whisk for 5–8 minutes until very thick and foamy, and the custard leaves a trail when the whisk is lifted above the mixture.

Drain off some of the cherry syrup, then tip the cherries and just a little of the syrup into a small saucepan. Warm through, then spoon into dessert glasses.

Pour the warm zabaglione over the top and decorate with the crumbled amaretti. Serve immediately.

# GINGER & HAZELNUT ICE CREAM

*Serves:* 4
*Prep time:* 5 minutes, plus freezing

300 ml (½ pint) double (heavy) cream
2 tablespoons milk
4 tablespoons icing (confectioners') sugar, sifted
50 g (2 oz) stem ginger, drained and finely chopped
4 teaspoons ginger syrup
2–4 tablespoons finely chopped hazelnuts, plus extra to decorate

Whip the cream and milk lightly, then fold in the icing sugar. Pour into a shallow freezer container, cover and freeze for about 45 minutes, until the mixture has frozen around the sides of the container.

Turn into a chilled bowl and whisk until smooth. Stir in the ginger, ginger syrup and hazelnuts.

Return the mixture to the container, cover and freeze until firm. Transfer to the refrigerator about 20 minutes before serving, to soften.

Scoop into dishes and sprinkle with a few extra chopped hazelnuts to serve.

# SHOWSTOPPERS

# APPLE CAKE

VG

*Serves:* 8
*Prep time:* 20 minutes
*Cook time:* 1¼ hours

- vegan margarine, for greasing
- 350 g (11½ oz) self-raising flour
- ½ teaspoon bicarbonate of soda (baking soda)
- ½ teaspoon fine sea salt
- 1 teaspoon ground cinnamon (optional)
- 3–4 apples (about 350 g / 11½ oz), peeled, cored and chopped into 1–1.5 cm (½–¾ inch) chunks, plus extra (optional) for topping
- 75 g (3 oz) sultanas or raisins (optional)
- 50 g (2 oz) hazelnuts, chopped (optional)
- finely grated zest and juice of ½ lemon
- 75 ml (3 fl oz) vegetable oil
- 225 ml (7½ fl oz) dairy-free milk
- 2 tablespoons demerara sugar (optional)

Grease a 20 cm (8 inch) loose-bottomed cake tin (cake pan) and line the base with nonstick baking paper.

In a large bowl, combine the flour, bicarbonate of soda, salt and cinnamon, if using. Toss in the apple chunks, sultanas or raisins and hazelnuts, if using, and coat them all thoroughly in the flour mixture.

In a smaller separate bowl, mix together the lemon zest and juice, oil and milk. Slowly add the wet ingredients to the dry and fold them in using a large spoon or spatula until fully combined.

Spoon the batter into the prepared tin, smoothing out the top. You can use one-quarter of an apple, very thinly sliced, laid out in a spiral shape on top of your cake, if you like. Sprinkle the sugar over the top, if using. Bake in a preheated oven, 160°C (325°F), Gas Mark 3, for 1¼ hours until a skewer inserted into the centre comes out clean.

Allow to cool for 15 minutes in the tin before removing the sides of the loose-bottomed tin and popping the cake onto a wire rack. Serve slightly warm. It will keep in an airtight container for up to 6 days.

# CHOCOLATE & BEETROOT FUDGE CAKE

(VG)

*Serves:* 12
*Prep time:* 20 minutes, plus cooling and chilling
*Cook time:* 45–50 minutes

250 g (8 oz) plain (all-purpose) flour

75 g (3 oz) cocoa powder

1 teaspoon bicarbonate of soda (baking soda)

300 g (10½ oz) light muscovado (brown) sugar

250 g (8 oz) cooked fresh beetroot (beets), chopped

300 ml (½ pint) almond milk

100 ml (3½ fl oz) sunflower oil, plus extra for oiling

2 teaspoons vanilla extract

1 tablespoon cider vinegar

## FOR THE ICING

150 g (5 oz) vegan spread

225 g (8 oz) icing (confectioners') sugar

1 teaspoon vanilla extract

150 g (5 oz) dairy-free plain dark chocolate, melted and cooled

Sift the flour, cocoa powder and bicarbonate of soda together into a large bowl. Stir in the sugar and set aside.

Blend the beetroot in a blender or food processor until smooth. With the motor running, pour in the almond milk, oil, vanilla extract and vinegar.

Tip the blended beetroot into the dry ingredients and stir until thoroughly mixed. Pour the mixture into an oiled and base-lined 20 cm (8 inch) springform cake tin (cake pan). Bake in a preheated oven, 180°C (350°F), Gas Mark 4, for 45–50 minutes until just firm to the touch. Leave to cool in the tin.

Meanwhile, make the icing. Beat the spread, icing sugar and vanilla extract together in an electric mixer until soft, then gradually beat in the melted chocolate until well combined and smooth. Refrigerate for 1 hour. Release the cooled cake from the tin and spread with the chilled icing.

# Old-Fashioned Coffee Cake

*Serves:* 8
*Prep time:* 30 minutes
*Cook time:* 20 minutes

- 175 g (6 oz) margarine, plus extra for greasing
- 175 g (6 oz) light muscovado (brown) or caster (superfine) sugar
- 175 g (6 oz) self-raising flour
- 1 teaspoon baking powder
- 3 eggs
- 3 teaspoons instant coffee, dissolved in 2 teaspoons boiling water

### FOR THE FROSTING

- 75 g (3 oz) butter, at room temperature
- 150 g (5 oz) icing (confectioners') sugar, sifted
- 3 teaspoons instant coffee, dissolved in 2 teaspoons boiling water
- 50 g (2 oz) dark chocolate, melted

Beat all the cake ingredients in a mixing bowl or a food processor until smooth.

Divide the mixture evenly between 2 x 18 cm (7 inch) sandwich tins, greased and base-lined with oiled greaseproof paper (wax paper), and spread the surfaces level.

Bake in a preheated oven, 180°C (350°F), Gas Mark 4, for 20 minutes until well risen, the cakes are browned and spring back when gently pressed with a fingertip.

Leave the cakes for a few minutes, then loosen the edges, turn out onto a wire rack and peel off the lining paper. Leave to cool.

Make the frosting. Put the butter and half the icing sugar in a mixing bowl, add the dissolved coffee and beat until smooth. Gradually mix in the remaining icing sugar until pale and creamy.

Put one of the cakes on a serving plate, spread with half the frosting, then cover with the second cake. Spread the remaining frosting over the top.

Pipe or drizzle swirls of melted chocolate on top. This cake can be stored in a cake tin for 2–3 days in a cool place.

# COFFEE CAKE WITH PISTACHIO PRALINE

*Serves:* 12
*Prep time:* 40 minutes
*Cook time:* 30–35 minutes

6 eggs

175 g (6 oz) caster (superfine) sugar

175 g (6 oz) plain (all-purpose) flour, sifted

50 g (2 oz) butter, melted, plus extra for greasing

2 tablespoons espresso coffee, cooled

### FOR THE PRALINE

65 g (2½ oz) shelled pistachio nuts

125 g (4 oz) granulated sugar

50 ml (2 fl oz) water

### FOR THE MAPLE SYRUP ICING

6 egg yolks

175 g (6 oz) caster (superfine) sugar

150 ml (¼ pint) milk

375 g (12 oz) unsalted butter, at room temperature, diced

3 tablespoons maple syrup

Whisk the eggs and sugar in a heatproof bowl set over a saucepan of gently simmering water for 5 minutes until very thick and the whisk leaves a trail when lifted above the mixture. Remove from the heat, then fold in the flour, butter and coffee.

Transfer the mixture to an greased and base-lined 23 cm (9 inch) cake tin (cake pan). Bake in a preheated oven, 180°C (350°F), Gas Mark 4, for 25–30 minutes. Leave to cool in the tin for 5 minutes, then turn out onto a wire rack. Slice the cake horizontally into 3 layers.

Put the nuts on a baking sheet. Heat the sugar and measurement water in a heavy-based saucepan until the sugar dissolves. Increase the heat until the sugar turns light golden. Remove from the heat and pour over the nuts. Once set, break the praline into small pieces and then grind to a rough powder.

Make the icing. Beat the egg yolks and sugar together until pale. Heat the milk until just boiling, then whisk into the egg mixture. Return to the pan and heat gently, stirring, until the mixture coats the back of the spoon. Beat the mixture off the heat for 2–3 minutes and then gradually beat in the butter, a little at a time, until the mixture is thick and glossy. Beat in the maple syrup.

Fold half the praline into half the icing and use to sandwich the layers together. Spread the remaining icing over the top and sides of the cake and sprinkle with the reserved praline.

*Serves:* 10
*Prep time:* 20 minutes
*Cook time:* 45 minutes

# TOFFEE & CHOCOLATE CAKE

175 g (6 oz) plain (all-purpose) flour

25 g (1 oz) cocoa powder

½ teaspoon bicarbonate of soda (baking soda)

½ teaspoon baking powder

200 g (7 oz) light muscovado (brown) sugar

1 egg

4 tablespoons milk

1 teaspoon vanilla extract

65 g (2½ oz) lightly salted butter, diced, plus extra for greasing

100 g (3½ oz) plain dark chocolate, chopped

125 ml (4 fl oz) water

chocolate curls, to decorate

## FOR THE TOPPING

40 g (1½ oz) very soft unsalted butter

200 g (7 oz) ready-made caramel or toffee sauce

Mix together the flour, cocoa powder, bicarbonate of soda, baking powder and sugar in a bowl. Beat together the egg, milk and vanilla extract in a small bowl.

Put the butter, chocolate and measurement water in a saucepan and heat very gently, stirring frequently, until melted and smooth. Add the egg mixture, melted butter and chocolate mixture to the dry ingredients and stir well to mix.

Spoon the mixture into a greased and lined 23 cm (9 inch) round or 20 cm (8 inch) square cake tin (cake pan) and level the surface. Bake in a preheated oven, 180°C (350°F), Gas Mark 4, for 30–40 minutes until just firm to the touch and a skewer inserted into the centre comes out clean. Loosen the edges, turn out onto a wire rack and peel off the lining paper. Leave to cool.

Make the topping. Beat together the butter and caramel or toffee sauce in a bowl. Transfer the cake to a serving plate, spread the topping over the top of the cake and scatter with chocolate curls.

*Serves:* 10
*Prep time:* 40 minutes
*Cook time:* 25 minutes

# Carrot & Walnut Cake

- 150 ml (¼ pint) sunflower oil
- 3 eggs
- 175 g (6 oz) light muscovado (brown) sugar
- 175 g (6 oz) self-raising flour
- 1½ teaspoons baking powder
- grated rind of ½ orange
- 1 teaspoon ground cinnamon
- 150 g (5 oz) carrots, coarsely grated
- 50 g (2 oz) walnuts, finely chopped, plus 5 walnut halves, halved, to decorate

## FOR THE MAPLE FROSTING

- 250 ml (8 fl oz) maple syrup
- 2 egg whites
- pinch of salt

Put the oil, eggs and sugar in a mixing bowl and whisk together until smooth.

Add the flour, baking powder, orange rind and ground cinnamon and whisk again until smooth. Stir in the carrots and chopped nuts. Divide the mixture between 2 x 20 cm (8 inch) sandwich tins, greased and base-lined with greaseproof paper (wax paper), and level.

Bake in a preheated oven, 180°C (350°F), Gas Mark 4, for about 20 minutes until the tops spring back when pressed. Cool for 5 minutes in the tins, then turn out onto a wire rack and peel off the lining paper. Leave to cool.

Make the maple frosting. Pour the maple syrup into a saucepan and heat to 115°C (240°F) on a sugar thermometer. As the temperature begins to rise, whisk the egg whites and salt in a clean bowl until stiff. When the syrup is ready, whisk it into the egg whites in a thin trickle until the frosting is like a meringue mixture. Keep whisking for a few minutes more until very thick.

Cut each cake in half, then sandwich 4 layers together with frosting. Transfer to a serving plate, then swirl the rest of the frosting over the top and sides of the cake. Decorate the top with the walnut pieces.

# ST CLEMENTS CAKE

*Serves:* 8
*Prep time:* 30 minutes
*Cook time:* 20 minutes

175 g (6 oz) margarine, plis extra for greasing

175 g (6 oz) caster (superfine) sugar

175 g (6 oz) self-raising flour

1 teaspoon baking powder

3 eggs

finely grated rind of 1 lemon

finely grated rind of 1 orange

icing (confectioners') sugar, for dusting

**FOR THE FILLING**

3 tablespoons lemon curd

150 ml (¼ pint) double (heavy) cream, whipped

Beat all the cake ingredients in a mixing bowl or a food processor until smooth.

Spoon the cake mixture evenly into 2 greased and base-lined 18 cm (7 inch) sandwich tins and spread the surfaces level. Bake in a preheated oven, 180°C (350°F), Gas Mark 4, for 20 minutes until well risen, the cakes are golden brown and spring back when gently pressed with a fingertip.

Leave to cool in the tin for 5 minutes, then loosen the edges, turn out onto a wire rack and peel off the lining paper. Leave to cool.

Transfer one of the cakes to a serving plate and spread with the lemon curd. Spoon the whipped cream on top, then cover with the remaining cake. Dust the top of the cake lightly with icing sugar. This is best eaten on the day it is made.

# Chocolate Bombe Cake

*Serves:* 20
*Prep time:* 1 hour, plus cooling
*Cook time:* 1¼ hours

- 250 g (8 oz) butter, plus extra for greasing
- 250 g (8 oz) golden caster (superfine) sugar
- a few drops of vanilla extract
- 5 eggs, lightly beaten
- 250 g (8 oz) self-raising flour, plus extra for dusting
- 100 g (3½ oz) white chocolate chips
- 100 g (3½ oz) plain dark chocolate chips
- 25 g (1 oz) cocoa powder
- 75 g (3 oz) warm apricot jam (jelly)

### FOR THE SYRUP

- 50 g (2 oz) golden caster (superfine) sugar
- 100 ml (3½ fl oz) water
- 50 ml (2 fl oz) orange liqueur

### FOR THE MARZIPAN

- 1 tablespoon orange liqueur
- 50 g (2 oz) cocoa powder
- 450 g (14½ oz) white marzipan

Cream together the butter, sugar and vanilla extract until pale and fluffy, then gradually beat in the eggs. Fold in the flour. Spoon half the mixture into a separate bowl. Add the white chocolate chips to 1 bowl and the plain dark chocolate chips and cocoa powder to the other. Mix each until combined.

Grease a 23 cm (9 inch) dome-shaped tin or heatproof bowl and dust with flour. Spoon in the mixtures alternately, then run a knife through them to create a marble effect. Bake in a preheated oven, 180°C (350°F), Gas Mark 4, for 1–1¼ hours. Leave in the tin for 15 minutes, then turn out onto a wire rack and cool for a further 30 minutes.

Make the syrup. Boil the sugar and measurement water in a saucepan until the liquid becomes syrupy. Remove from the heat and add the liqueur.

For the marzipan, knead the liqueur and cocoa powder into the marzipan. Roll out two-thirds between 2 sheets of nonstick baking paper to a 40 cm (16 inch) circle, then mould large ripples across it by using your fingertips to gently pinch and pull sections of the marzipan upwards.

Turn the cake onto a serving plate. Spoon over the syrup and brush with apricot jam. Drape the marzipan over and trim off the excess at the base. Pat the sides to make an edge.

Roll out the remaining marzipan and cut 20 x 2.5 cm (1 inch) flower shapes. Arrange the small flowers at the base of the cake.

# CHOCOLATE FUDGE RING

*Serves:* 12
*Prep time:* 20 minutes, plus cooling
*Cook time:* 40 minutes

175 g (6 oz) self-raising flour
50 g (2 oz) cocoa powder
2 teaspoons baking powder
175 g (6 oz) caster (superfine) sugar
175 g (6 oz) butter, plus extra for greasing
4 eggs
2 teaspoons vanilla extract
4 tablespoons milk
walnut halves, to decorate

### FOR THE ICING

300 g (10 oz) plain dark chocolate, broken into pieces
4 tablespoons milk
50 g (2 oz) butter
225 g (7½ oz) icing (confectioners') sugar, plus extra for dusting

Sift the flour, cocoa powder and baking powder into a bowl. Add the sugar, butter, eggs, vanilla extract and milk and whisk until they are evenly combined.

Grease and line the base of a 1.8 litre (3 pint) ring cake tin (cake pan). Turn the mixture into the tin and level the surface. Bake in a preheated oven, 180°C (350°F), Gas Mark 4, for 35 minutes, or until just firm to the touch. Use a palette knife to loosen the cake from the side of the tin, then invert the cake onto a wire rack and leave to cool.

Make the icing. Heat the chocolate gently in a heavy-based saucepan with the milk until it has melted, stirring frequently. Stir in the butter. Beat in the icing sugar and leave the mixture to cool slightly.

Cut the cake horizontally into 3 layers. Beat the icing again until it has a slightly fudge-like texture. Use a little icing to sandwich the layers together. Spread the remaining icing over the top and sides of the cake, swirling it with a palette knife. Decorate the top of the cake with the walnut halves and dust with icing sugar.

# Very Rich Chocolate Gateau

*Serves:* 12–14

*Prep time:* 25 minutes, plus cooling and setting

*Cook time:* 40 minutes

200 g (7 oz) plain dark chocolate

2 tablespoons milk

175 g (6 oz) butter, plus extra for greasing

175 g (6 oz) caster (superfine) sugar

175 g (6 oz) ground hazelnuts or almonds

40 g (1½ oz) plain (all-purpose) flour

5 eggs, separated

3 tablespoons hot water

### FOR THE SYRUP

25 g (1 oz) caster (superfine) sugar

4 tablespoons brandy or orange/coffee liqueur

50 ml (2 fl oz) water

### FOR THE GLAZE

5 tablespoons apricot jam (jelly)

25 g (1 oz) caster (superfine) sugar

75 ml (3 fl oz) water

200 g (7 oz) plain dark chocolate

25 g (1 oz) milk chocolate

Melt the plain dark chocolate with the milk in a bowl over a pan of simmering water. Put the chocolate mixture, butter, sugar, hazelnuts or almonds, flour and egg yolks in a bowl with the hot water and beat until smooth.

Whisk the egg whites until peaking, then fold them into the chocolate mixture.

Grease and line a 23 cm (9 inch) cake tin (cake pan). Pour the mixture into the tin and level. Bake in a preheated oven, 180°C (350°F), Gas Mark 4, for about 30 minutes until just firm. Cover with a damp tea towel (cloth kitchen towel) and leave to cool.

Make the syrup. Mix the sugar, the brandy or liqueur and measurement water in a small saucepan and heat gently until the sugar dissolves. Boil rapidly for 1 minute until syrupy. Invert the cake onto a wire rack, remove the lining paper and spoon the syrup over the top.

Make the glaze. Heat the jam, press through a sieve (strainer) and brush over the cake. Heat the caster sugar in a small, heavy-based saucepan with the measurement water until the sugar has dissolved. Boil rapidly for 1 minute. Remove from the heat, leave for 1 minute, then stir in the plain dark chocolate. Stir frequently until melted. Leave until beginning to thicken. Melt the milk chocolate.

Pour the chocolate glaze over the cake, easing it down the side with a palette knife. Drizzle the milk chocolate around the top edges of the cake to give a decorative finish. Leave in a cool place to set.

# HAZELNUT MERINGUE GATEAU

*Serves:* 8–10
*Prep time:* 30 minutes, plus cooling and chilling
*Cook time:* 1–1¼ hours

- 5 eggs, separated
- 300 g (10 oz) caster (superfine) sugar
- 1 tablespoon cornflour (cornstarch)
- 125 g (4 oz) blanched hazelnuts, toasted and finely ground
- 250 g (8 oz) plain dark chocolate, broken into pieces
- 200 ml (7 fl oz) double (heavy) cream
- cocoa powder, for dusting

### FOR THE CHOCOLATE HAZELNUTS

- 50 g (2 oz) plain dark chocolate, broken into pieces
- 50 g (2 oz) hazelnuts

Line 3 baking sheets and draw a 23 cm (9 inch) circle on each piece of baking paper.

Whisk the egg whites until stiff, then gradually whisk in the sugar until thick and glossy. Fold in the cornflour and ground hazelnuts until evenly incorporated and transfer the mixture to a large piping bag fitted with a 1 cm (⅓ inch) plain nozzle. Starting in the centre of each prepared circle, pipe the mixture in a continuous coil, finishing just within the marked line.

Bake in a preheated oven, 150°C (300°F), Gas Mark 2, for 1–1¼ hours until lightly golden and dried out. Remove from the oven and transfer to a wire rack to cool completely. Peel away the baking paper.

Melt the chocolate together with the cream over a pan of gently simmering water to make the filling. Cool, then chill for 1 hour until thickened.

Make the chocolate hazelnuts. Melt the chocolate and use a fork to dip in the hazelnuts until coated. Leave to set on baking paper.

Beat the chocolate filling until it is light and fluffy and use to sandwich the meringue layers together.

Decorate the gateau with the chocolate hazelnuts and serve dusted with cocoa powder.

# RICH CHRISTMAS CAKE

*Serves:* 16
*Prep time:* 45 minutes, plus cooling
*Cook time:* 3–3½ hours

125 g (4 oz) self-raising flour
200 g (7 oz) plain (all-purpose) flour
¼ teaspoon salt
1 teaspoon ground mixed spice
½ teaspoon ground cinnamon
½ teaspoon ground nutmeg
250 g (8 oz) butter, plus extra for greasing
250 g (8 oz) soft dark brown or dark muscovado (brown) sugar
2 teaspoons black treacle (molasses)
5 eggs
50 ml (2 fl oz) medium-dry sherry or strained cold tea
1½ teaspoons vanilla extract
250 g (8 oz) currants
250 g (8 oz) sultanas
250 g (8 oz) seedless raisins
250 g (8 oz) prunes or dates, roughly chopped
75 g (3 oz) mixed peel
50 g (2 oz) ground almonds (almond meal)
75 g (3 oz) glacé cherries, halved
finely grated rind of 1 lemon
3–4 tablespoons brandy

Grease and line a 23 cm (9 inch) round or 20 cm (8 inch) square cake tin (cake pan), using a double thickness of greaseproof paper (wax paper). Line the outside with several thicknesses of brown paper, standing at least 5 cm (2 inches) above the top of the tin.

Sift the flours into a large bowl with the salt, mixed spice, cinnamon and nutmeg. In another large bowl, cream the butter with the sugar until light. Beat in the treacle.

Lightly beat together the eggs, sherry or tea and vanilla extract. Gradually beat half the egg mixture into the creamed mixture. Fold in one-third of the mixed flours. Continue to add the egg and flour mixtures alternately. Mix in all the remaining ingredients except the brandy. Pour into the prepared tin and smooth the top.

Bake in a preheated oven, 140°C (275°F), Gas Mark 1, for 3–3½ hours until a skewer inserted into the centre of the cake comes out clean. Cover the cake with a double layer of greaseproof paper if it starts to brown too much during cooking.

Leave the cake to cool in the tin before turning out onto a wire rack to cool completely. Prick all over with a fine skewer and spoon brandy over the cake. Store the cake in an airtight tin and leave to mature for about 1 month before using.

# Chocolate & Chestnut Roulade

*Serves:* 8

*Prep time:* 15 minutes, plus cooling and chilling

*Cook time:* 20 minutes

- butter, for greasing
- 6 eggs, separated
- 125 g (4 oz) caster (superfine) sugar
- 2 tablespoons cocoa powder
- 150 ml (¼ pint) whipping cream
- 100 g (3½ oz) chestnut purée or sweetened chestnut spread
- icing (confectioners') sugar, for dusting

Grease and line a 29 x 18 cm (11½ x 7 inch) Swiss roll tin. Whisk the egg whites in a large clean bowl until they form soft peaks. Put the egg yolks and sugar in a separate bowl and whisk together until thick and pale. Fold in the cocoa powder and the egg whites, then tip into the prepared tin.

Bake in a preheated oven, 180°C (350°F), Gas Mark 4, for 20 minutes. Leave to cool in the tin, then tip out onto a piece of greaseproof paper (wax paper) that has been dusted with icing sugar.

Pour the cream into a large clean bowl and whisk until it forms soft peaks. Fold the chestnut purée or spread into the cream, then smooth the mixture over the roulade.

Using the greaseproof paper to help you, carefully roll up the roulade from one short end and lift it gently onto a serving dish (do not worry if it cracks). Dust with icing sugar. Chill until needed and eat on the day it is made.

# Pear, Cinnamon & Raisin Kugelhopf

*Makes:* 1 ring loaf
*Prep time:* 30 minutes, plus proving and shaping
*Cook time:* 35–40 minutes

## FOR THE DOUGH

- 375 g (12 oz) strong white bread flour, plus extra for dusting
- 50 g (2 oz) caster (superfine) sugar
- 1 teaspoon fast-action dried yeast
- ½ teaspoon salt
- 150 ml (¼ pint) strong cider
- 1 large egg, beaten
- 75 g (3 oz) unsalted butter, melted

## FOR THE FILLING

- 50 g (2 oz) unsalted butter, softened
- 75 g (3 oz) dark muscovado (brown) sugar
- 2 teaspoons ground cinnamon
- 4 ripe pears
- 2 teaspoons lemon juice
- 100 g (3½ oz) raisins
- icing (confectioners') sugar, for dusting

Put the dry dough ingredients in a mixing bowl and stir. Make a hollow in the centre and add the cider and egg and mix together. Tip the mixture on a floured surface and knead the dough until it becomes soft, smooth and elastic. Add the butter a little at a time and continue to knead for 5–8 minutes until thoroughly combined.

Place the dough in a large, clean bowl, cover with clingfilm (plastic wrap) and chill in the refrigerator until it has doubled in size (preferably overnight).

Make the filling. Mix the butter with the sugar and cinnamon to make a paste. Peel, core and slice the pears. Toss in the lemon juice to prevent browning.

Remove the dough from the refrigerator and turn it out onto a floured surface and roll out into a rectangle, about 35 x 25 cm (14 x 10 inches). Spread the spiced butter over the dough almost to the edges and scatter with the pears and raisins. Loosely roll up the dough. With the join facing upwards, bring the ends of the dough to meet and press them together. Thoroughly grease and flour the base and sides of a 1.5 litre (2½ pint) kugelhopf tin or plain ring tin. Place the dough into the tin.

Cover loosely with oiled clingfilm and leave to rise in a warm place for 50–60 minutes, or until the dough has risen to the top of the tin.

Bake in a preheated oven, 200°C (400°F), Gas Mark 6, for about 35 minutes until risen and deep golden. Leave in the tin for 10 minutes, then loosen the edges with a knife and invert onto a wire rack to cool. Serve warm or cold, dusted with icing sugar.

# INDEX


## A

amaretti & chocolate custard 196
apples
- apple & blackberry strudels 29
- apple & cinnamon muffins 63
- apple & hazelnut filos 21
- apple cake 214
- apple fritters 13
- apple, maple & pecan fool 203
- caramel crumble 183
- cidered apple & fig loaf 85
- deep dish puff apple pie 43
- hot blackberry & apple trifle 176
- mincemeat & apple pies 34
- mincemeat & apple strudel 29
- spicy apple parkin 128
- steamed apple pudding 171
- sticky toffee apples 161
- toffee apple mini traybakes 124
- toffee apple tarts 52

apricot & blueberry cobbler 187
apricot & pistachio purses 18

## B

baked chocolate cheesecake 190
baked honey, cardamom & cinnamon figs 159
bananas
- banana fritters 13
- banana, date & walnut loaf 87
- banoffee chocolate muffins 58
- banoffee meringues 160
- banoffee pie 189
- caramel & banana bread pudding 164

beetroot
- chocolate & beetroot fudge cake 216

berries
- caramelized berry rice pudding 187

blackberries
- apple & blackberry strudels 29
- hot blackberry & apple trifle 176

blueberries
- apricot & blueberry cobbler 187
- spicy fruit bread puddings 169

boozy ginger chocs 145
bran
- sticky sultana & bran slice 87

brandied prune & custard tart 48
bread & butter pudding, chocolate 163
bread pudding, caramel & banana 164
bread puddings, spicy fruit 169
butter
- chocolate bread & butter pudding 163
- cinnamon butter fancies 80

butterscotch sauce 209

## C

cappuccino cupcakes 63
caramel
- caramel & banana bread pudding 164
- caramel & honeycomb mousse 206
- caramel chocolate fondants 174
- caramel crumble 183
- caramel ice cream cake 179
- caramel pear tarte Tatin 34
- caramel pine nut slice 134
- caramelized berry rice pudding 187
- caramelized nuts 152
- salted caramel crunch brownies 118
- salted caramel shards 151
- slow cooker crème caramels 200

cardamom
- baked honey, cardamom & cinnamon figs 159
- chocolate & cardamom pots 199
- clove & cardamom cookies 104
- lemon & cardamom cupcakes 65
- pear, cardamom & sultana cake 89

carrot & walnut cake 223
carrot & walnut cupcakes 77
cherries
- cherry & cinnamon zabaglione 211
- cinnamon-spiced cherries 179
- sweet cherry pies 35

chestnuts
- chocolate & chestnut roulade 236

chilli chocolate chip muffins 58
chocolate
- amaretti & chocolate custard 196
- baked chocolate cheesecake 190
- banoffee chocolate muffins 58
- boozy ginger chocs 145
- caramel chocolate fondants 174
- chilli chocolate chip muffins 58
- chocolate & beetroot fudge cake 216
- chocolate & cardamom pots 199
- chocolate & chestnut roulade 236
- chocolate & chestnut roulade 236
- chocolate & chestnut roulade 236
- chocolate & ginger tart 49
- chocolate & gingernut mousse 207
- chocolate & pistachio soufflés 180
- chocolate bombe cake 227
- chocolate bread & butter pudding 163
- chocolate chip cookies 101
- chocolate cream pie 184
- chocolate filigree torte 32
- chocolate fudge ring 229
- chocolate iced fancies 82
- chocolate orange madeleines 92
- chocolate peanut butter whoopie pies 99
- chocolate puddle pudding 170
- chocolate raspberry friands 93
- chocolate ripple loaf 74
- chocolate sea salt cupcakes 60
- chocolate toffee popcorn 152
- classic chocolate brownies 116
- coffee chocolate bavarois 204
- florentines 112
- frying pan chocolate brownies 116
- ginger & chocolate cookies 109
- glazed chocolate ginger hearts 147
- hazelnut meringue gateau 232
- jaffa orange fudge 142

mile-high chocolate meringue pie 36
mini chocolate logs 119
mint & chocolate fudge 142
peanut butter millionaire's shortbread 106
pecan, maple syrup & chocolate tart 51
rich chocolate macaroons 96
rocky road clusters 140
toffee & chocolate cake 221
triple chocolate biscotti 103
triple chocolate cupcakes 68
very rich chocolate gateau 230
walnut & white chocolate cookies 100
white chocolate & nut blondies 114
white chocolate & strawberry cheesecake 199
white chocolate torte 45
choux pastry
gingered profiteroles 26
toffee choux buns 25
Christmas cake 235
Christmas pudding parfait with butterscotch 209
churros, quick 14
cidered apple & fig loaf 85
cinnamon
apple & cinnamon muffins 63
baked honey, cardamom & cinnamon figs 159
cherry & cinnamon zabaglione 211
cinnamon butter fancies 80
cinnamon doughnuts 17
cinnamon-spiced cherries 179
cinnamon sugar muffins 66
cinnamon tarts 49
glazed pear & cinnamon loaf 88
honey, grape & cinnamon tartlets 53
orange & cinnamon puddings 173
pan-fried peach & plum cinnamon crunch 159
peachy cinnamon cheesecake 193
pear, cinnamon & raisin kugelhopf 239
ricotta with warm cinnamon honey 203
speedy cinnamon rolls 16
sticky cinnamon & pecan buns 10
classic chocolate brownies 116
clove & cardamom cookies 104
coffee
cappuccino cupcakes 63
coffee cake with pistachio praline 220
coffee chocolate bavarois 204
marbled coffee cupcakes 69
marsala raisin coffee muffins 61
old-fashioned coffee cake 219
cookies
milk & cookie brownies 114
cranberries
sweet cranberry & orange pie 38
cream
banoffee pie 189
creamy pistachio toffee 145
nectarine brûlée 193
vanilla crème brûlée 194
cream cheese
baked chocolate cheesecake 190
chocolate cream pie 184
peachy cinnamon cheesecake 193
custard
amaretti & chocolate custard 196
brandied prune & custard tart 48
hot blackberry & apple trifle 176

# D

dates
banana, date & walnut loaf 87
date & pistachio truffles 151
date & sesame bars 132
date crescents 24
maple syrup, date & pecan puddings 173
sticky toffee & date loaf 84
sticky toffee & date squares 126
deep dish puff apple pie 43

# F

figs
baked honey, cardamom & cinnamon figs 159
cidered apple & fig loaf 85
iced fig slice 135
florentines 112
fruit, dried
florentines 112
mulled wine biscuits 120
panforte di Siena 131
rich Christmas cake 235
spicy fruit bread puddings 169
frying pan chocolate brownies 116

# G

gâteau Pithiviers with plums 22
ginger
boozy ginger chocs 145
chocolate & ginger tart 49
ginger & chocolate cookies 109
ginger & hazelnut ice cream 211
ginger & treacle sponge pudding 169
gingerbread people 109
gingered profiteroles 26
gingered treacle tart 46
glazed chocolate ginger hearts 147
honey & ginger flapjacks 137
Jamaican ginger cake 81
orange, rhubarb & ginger slump 183
pomegranate & ginger slice 79
spiced ginger cupcakes 56
sticky gingerbread 129
gingernut biscuits
chocolate & gingernut mousse 207
glazed chocolate ginger hearts 147
glazed pear & cinnamon loaf 88
golden syrup
ginger & treacle sponge pudding 169
gingered treacle tart 46
steamed puddings with golden syrup 164
tiny treacle tarts 33
grapes
honey, grape & cinnamon tartlets 53

# H

hazelnuts
apple & hazelnut filos 21
ginger & hazelnut ice cream 211
hazelnut meringue gateau 232
hazelnut meringues 148
spiced hazelnut palmiers 21
honey
baked honey, cardamom & cinnamon figs 159

honey & ginger flapjacks 137
honey halva griwech 14
honey, grape & cinnamon tartlets 53
honeyed pecan pie 42
ricotta with warm cinnamon honey 203
honeycomb
caramel & honeycomb mousse 206
hot blackberry & apple trifle 176


# I


ice cream
caramel ice cream cake 179
ginger & hazelnut ice cream 211
iced fig slice 135


# J


jaffa orange fudge 142
Jamaican ginger cake 81


# L


layered nutty bars 132
lemons
lemon & cardamom cupcakes 65
St Clements cake 224


# M


macadamias
maple syrup & macadamia madeleines 90
maple syrup
apple, maple & pecan fool 203
carrot & walnut cake 223
coffee cake with pistachio praline 220
maple & pecan muffins 66
maple biscuits 111
maple syrup & macadamia madeleines 90
maple syrup, date & pecan puddings 173
pecan, maple syrup & chocolate tart 51
marbled coffee cupcakes 69
marsala raisin coffee muffins 61
marshmallow crackle squares 137
marzipan
marzipan cupcakes 71
stollen slice 73
meringue
banoffee meringues 160
hazelnut meringue gateau 232
hazelnut meringues 148
mile-high chocolate meringue pie 36
spiced pumpkin meringue pie 40
mile-high chocolate meringue pie 36
milk
milk & cookie brownies 114
slow cooker crème caramels 200
mincemeat
mince pie cupcakes 76
mincemeat & apple pies 34
mincemeat & apple strudel 29
mincemeat muffins 69
mini chocolate logs 119
mint & chocolate fudge 142
mulled wine biscuits 120


# N


nectarine brûlée 193
nuts
caramelized nuts 152
florentines 112
layered nutty bars 132
mulled wine biscuits 120
panforte di Siena 131
rocky road clusters 140
white chocolate & nut blondies 114


# O


old-fashioned coffee cake 219
oranges
chocolate orange madeleines 92
orange & cinnamon puddings 173
orange, rhubarb & ginger slump 183
St Clements cake 224
sweet cranberry & orange pie 38


# P


pan-fried peach & plum cinnamon crunch 159
panforte di Siena 131
peaches
pan-fried peach & plum cinnamon crunch 159
peachy cinnamon cheesecake 193
peanut butter
chocolate peanut butter whoopie pies 99
peanut butter & chocolate muffins 80
peanut butter cookies 104
peanut butter millionaire's shortbread 106
peanut cupcakes 74
pears
caramel pear tarte Tatin 34
glazed pear & cinnamon loaf 88
pear, cardamom & sultana cake 89
pear, cinnamon & raisin kugelhopf 239
roasted pears with sugar & spice 156
tarte Tatin with mulled pears 30
pecans
apple, maple & pecan fool 203
honeyed pecan pie 42
maple & pecan muffins 66
maple syrup, date & pecan puddings 173
pecan, maple syrup & chocolate tart 51
sticky cinnamon & pecan buns 10
pine nuts
caramel pine nut slice 134
pine nut praline 148
pistachios
apricot & pistachio purses 18
chocolate & pistachio soufflés 180
coffee cake with pistachio praline 220
creamy pistachio toffee 145
date & pistachio truffles 151
pistachio nut stollen 123
plums
gâteau Pithiviers with plums 22
pan-fried peach & plum cinnamon crunch 159
plum turnovers 24
pomegranate & ginger slice 79
popcorn
chocolate toffee popcorn 152
prunes
brandied prune & custard tart 48

pumpkin
  pumpkin pie 39
  spiced pumpkin meringue pie 40
pumpkin spice cupcakes 70

## Q

quick churros 14

## R

raisins
  marsala raisin coffee muffins 61
  pear, cinnamon & raisin kugelhopf 239
raspberries
  chocolate raspberry friands 93
rhubarb
  orange, rhubarb & ginger slump 183
rice pudding, caramelized berry 187
rich chocolate macaroons 96
rich Christmas cake 235
ricotta with warm cinnamon honey 203
roasted pears with sugar & spice 156
rocky road clusters 140

## S

salt
  chocolate sea salt cupcakes 60
  salted caramel crunch brownies 118
  salted caramel shards 151
sesame seeds
  date & sesame bars 132
slow cooker crème caramels 200
speedy cinnamon rolls 16
spices
  pumpkin spice cupcakes 70
  rich Christmas cake 235
  roasted pears with sugar & spice 156
  spiced ginger cupcakes 56
  spiced hazelnut palmiers 21
  spiced pumpkin meringue pie 40
  spiced sweet potato cupcakes 64
  spicy apple parkin 128
  spicy fruit bread puddings 169
St Clements cake 224
steamed apple pudding 171
steamed puddings with golden syrup 164
sticky cinnamon & pecan buns 10
sticky gingerbread 129
sticky sultana & bran slice 87
sticky toffee & date loaf 84
sticky toffee & date squares 126
sticky toffee apples 161
sticky toffee puddings 166
stollen slice 73
strawberries
  white chocolate & strawberry cheesecake 199
sultanas
  pear, cardamom & sultana cake 89
  sticky sultana & bran slice 87
sweet cherry pies 35
sweet cranberry & orange pie 38
sweet potato
  spiced sweet potato cupcakes 64

## T

tarte Tatin with mulled pears 30
tiny treacle tarts 33
toffee
  banoffee pie 189
  chocolate toffee popcorn 152
  creamy pistachio toffee 145
  sticky toffee & date loaf 84
  sticky toffee & date squares 126
  sticky toffee apples 161
  sticky toffee puddings 166
  toffee & chocolate cake 221
  toffee apple mini traybakes 124
  toffee apple tarts 52
  toffee choux buns 25
triple chocolate biscotti 103
triple chocolate cupcakes 68

## V

vanilla crème brûlée 194
very rich chocolate gateau 230

## W

walnuts
  banana, date & walnut loaf 87
  carrot & walnut cake 223
  carrot & walnut cupcakes 77
  walnut & white chocolate cookies 100
white chocolate & nut blondies 114
white chocolate & strawberry cheesecake 199
white chocolate torte 45
wine
  mulled wine biscuits 120